The Wisdom of Michael

Messages from an Archangel

A channeled book by Ron Head

ISBN 10: 1514618419

ISBN 13: 9781514618417

Introduction

A word on how this book has come into being. I began this journey into what we call spirituality in 1969 when I was living in Okinawa, Japan. At the time, it was a U.S. protectorate and I was in the Air Force. I lived there for four years, became a Buddhist, and had a new friend introduce me to a new world of reading and study that completely changed my view of life.

I have read, over the last forty-five years, thousands of books on a great many topics. I am not one who can remember titles, authors, or even all the subjects that I read about. But I know that my life has been thoroughly remade by all of it. For years, it seemed that there were many, many people in the world involved in this evolution of thought that we term 'new age' or 'new thought', but that I would never know any of them. It seemed that many of them had abilities that I would not have. It seemed that I was isolated from the entire thing in my own little backwater of the world. I lived in a city of millions, and yet I knew no one with whom I could discuss such things.

Events in my life led me to become a Reiki practitioner in the 1990s, and in 2009 I became a ThetaHealer®. It opened me up to a new level of consciousness, but still I seemed to be connected to this world of thought only by a new development called internet. I had joined Facebook and Skype in order to find other ThetaHealers® and clients. In January of 2012, one of those whom I had met this way, Suzanne Spooner, now a dear friend and mentor, began teaching her method of channeling called TAUK online for $20.12. I thought that was cute and that perhaps it would open me up a bit more. Little did I know.

Soon I was conversing daily with my guide, whom I knew as Amsah. Not long after that, because the messages were being spelled out word by word, Amsah put me through a week long nightly practice of intuiting the words and sentences I was getting by the context. I found myself getting better and better at it very quickly. I realize now that I was being given practice in telepathic channeling. But I did not yet know the purpose of it.

About the middle of February, 2012, Amsah ended his message to me by saying, "I have someone I want you to meet." I agreed and he said, "This is Michael." I was a mite taken aback by what followed. I was told that I needed to stop posting political and joking memes on Facebook, that it was not the sort of image that would be needed for the type of thing that Michael and I would be doing. I was told that there was much work to do, and that it was time to get started. I was told that I had to work on my bad attitude. Michael was not messing around. There were things to do and I needed to get ready to do them.

Shortly thereafter, I received a message through Michael that seemed not to be aimed at me personally. I asked what to do with it, and I was told, "Publish it." That confused me and I asked, "How? Do you want me to start a blog?" The answer was, "Yes."

Well, at the time, I had no idea how to start a blog. I mentioned this to Suzanne Spooner while chatting on Facebook and she said that a friend had helped her set up a WordPress blog and that she could set one up like it for me if I wished. The next thing I knew, I was posting the message I had received to my very own blog, and was soon posting every day.

Those first messages were, I think, highly colored by my own beliefs and desires, but still, they were also a necessary period of learning as I grew in my ability to channel and in getting and keeping myself clear. I hope and believe that what has come through me in the months that have followed is much more spirit and much less Ron. I am gratified that a great number of people from around the world have written to tell me how helpful it has been for them.

More than a few have expressed that they would enjoy having a book of the compiled messages, and this is the first attempt to create one. I am very lucky to have a dear friend, Annette Despain, helping me in this effort. She is also a ThetaHealer® and channel and is proving to be invaluable to the process, a true friend indeed.

We hope you enjoy what we have compiled. It is our intention and our heartfelt prayer that what we have put together here will aid you on your journey.

You will notice that there are breaks signified by lines of asterisks. These are to show the actual endings and beginnings of separate channeled messages. We have done this to keep the context intact and have only sorted these messages into broad categories. The hope is also that this may make finding certain subjects easier for the reader.

Table of Contents

CHANNELING

It is a wonderful thing and great gift you are being given.

It is our purpose this morning to discuss with you your opening to communications of these kinds. In your rising states of consciousness, it is becoming more and more common for you who think of yourselves as lightworkers to discover that, in one form or another, you can become the recipient of our thoughts. This is a wonderful occasion which we enjoy quite as much as you do yourselves.

There is, however, a tendency to be so enthusiastic in the discovery that the simple basics of personal protection are forgotten or left unlearned. There will come a time in the near future when that is not a problem, as negative energies and beings are just no longer a possibility where you are living. Regrettably, however, this is not yet the case.

Every reliable teacher of methods to begin these types of communication includes information urging beginners to clear themselves and their surroundings, and most are wise enough to urge their students to always begin each session, or each day, by reaching at least as high as the divine level of consciousness before allowing any communication to take place.

We can tell you that far too many are either ignoring these instructions or lack any experience of having heard them. They are being taken advantage of in all sorts of ways, up to and including allowing other beings to control their precious bodies and minds.

As fewer and fewer of these lower or negative beings continue to survive in the increasingly high frequencies of your surroundings, they are becoming more and more, shall we say, desperate to hold on. Many of your dear healers are being approached almost daily with these sorts of problems.

Firstly, dear ones, drop your fear. There are no conditions or problems that cannot be healed, cleared, changed. Seek the help of those who know what to do.

But our point this day is to urge you as strongly as possible to, at the very first sign that you are becoming telepathic, clairvoyant, or clairaudient, and this will be happening soon for large numbers of you, seek out that information which will keep you protected from negativity and the influence of those you do not want to be influenced by.

At this time, we wish to inform you that the method, which is of the very most effectiveness, is for you to begin by going, in meditation, to the very highest source that you can imagine. Learn to find your way to the even higher divine levels than our own. Go to the Creator of All. It matters not by what name you call this being, this energy. Source, Creator, Allah, Buddha, all will do, and other names as well. Reach the level of love and consciousness that has created the All That Is. And there learn to specify whom and what you wish to communicate with.

You are not participating in parlor games here. Your very soul can be involved and that is a serious thing. But we do NOT want to scare you with this. It is a wonderful thing and great gift you are being given. But just as if it were a higher-powered vehicle, which is what it is we suppose, some caution and responsibility is in order.

If you are among those who are currently beginning to notice these kinds of openings in yourselves, let us congratulate you and say that we look forward to working with you in every way possible. Approaching this in the proper way can be both enlightening and enjoyable. The joy and love that awaits you will be, we promise, well worth the effort. There are many, many who look forward to working with you.

Please do not be deterred by our words, but please also do not forget them.

* * * * * * * * * * *

We return today to the subject of channeling.

You should be noticing several things about the messages you are reading at this time. The first is that the messages contained therein are becoming clearer and clearer. You should also be seeing that there is a distinct difference between those that uplift your spirit and those that leave you confused or dejected. We hope you are giving no attention at all to any that bring forth fear.

Next you will be more and more surprised at the response you feel within. This is a direct result of both the love energy that is bringing about changes within yourselves and the allowance you are giving yourselves to change toward versions of yourselves that you

11

perceive as more desirable. You do know, after all, that you have put on a party face that you intended to disguise your true identity for this last act of the play. The time approaches for you to cast off the masks and take your bows. We are sure a standing ovation will be in order at that time.

But what we wish to bring to your attention this day, more forcefully perhaps than previously, is the continuing drawing together, or focus, of a great many of these channels upon a greater theme. Some of these, our messengers, do read others' material. Others steadfastly remain intentionally unaware of what the others are doing. Nevertheless, you will be able to see among all of them a greater focus on the inner world of your spirit and the metamorphosis that is occurring in your consciousness at this time. From this, please entertain the conclusion that they are drawing upon the One Consciousness and its most important underlying message to all. "Come home. Welcome home. We are one."

It is understood that this is in conflict with what you have been taught for centuries upon centuries, but you can see now that this message is beginning to take root in your world awareness. This is indeed the snowball, the avalanche, the unstoppable force of which we have spoken so very often.

Be at peace in your hearts now and allow this to take its course. Make this the day on which you relax into the loving arms of your Creator.

* * * * * * * * * * * *

We will begin a discussion this morning on the sources of channeled messages. We intend for this information to make it easier for those who find themselves in receipt of such messages to understand the process and trust what they receive.

Many more of you will find yourselves tuning in to vast fields of such information from this time forward. Your inner make-up is changing in such a way as to make this a part of your lives. You will receive rather more personal messages and some will also wish to be conduits for general information such as what has been recorded by this channel and others.

Understand that you are, and have always been, living in the midst of an ocean of frequencies carrying all of the information in the universes. This is exactly like the fact that you are sitting in a sea of radio and television signals which only proper equipment and tuners can intercept. You are the proper equipment for this new reception, and your tuners are being modified by the changes to each and all of you.

Some of this will require you to consciously volunteer yourselves, but much of the personal information will become available to you as you clear yourselves of old baggage and begin to open yourselves to the processes and understandings you call ascension.

As it has always been, some of you are visually oriented, some more feeling, some learn best through hearing, and some will do best by beginning to write each day and allowing the stream of thought to take you wherever it will. There is no right or wrong way to do this, with the following qualifications to that statement. If you are desirous of true, helpful, and trustworthy information to come forth, you must be of a matching energy to that. You will need to achieve a clarity and integrity of purpose and maintain it daily in order to keep information of clarity and integrity available to you. You will need to understand and accept your own responsibility and divine sovereignty, to assure that you and you alone have control of the process. Do not, we implore you, just fling the doors of your consciousness open to whatever happens to beg entry. Do not accept as absolute truth everything that you might hear, see, or think any more than you would do so in your outer world.

There are those who know and can aid you in learning how to handle all of the newfound gifts which you may acquire. All of that being said, let us get on to the topic we began with.

You may find that you can understand animals, trees, even your dear Mother Earth as you open up. You might find that certain formerly mythic beings become a bit less mythic for you. But of course those are not the subject of this discussion. What you will most certainly be able to find, if you so intend, is a connection with Spirit. You will have your own understandings of what that is for you to work through. Those various understandings have developed over the millennia and are deeply imbedded in your consciousness. And that is alright. You should begin to understand that a certain energy might be called by one name in your Orient and yet be known by quite another in your western cultures. I, Michael, assure you that none of us care by what name we are called. You have fought and killed each other over such things. Learn to discern the truth and use of the information and to give no importance to the vehicle and you will be far ahead of this new game. Well, new to you, perhaps, but actually very, very old. The fact is that it has always been around, but has been discouraged. Now the genie has been let out of the bottle, so to speak, and will not be put back in. Learn to use your inner abilities well, dear ones. We have waited a long time for you to begin hearing what we have always whispered to you. Listen well, and when you feel it is appropriate, share it with others.

* * * * * * * * * *

We wish to return today to one of our favorite topics, the phenomenon of channeled messages. You will have noticed a distinct change in the type, clarity, and, even in some instances the sources of these. What has changed? Have you given it any thought? More than a few of those involved in bringing these messages to you have done so. We bring this up today to illustrate a different, but related point. So we will spend a little time explaining and then we will connect the dots, as you say.

The changes that these messengers are experiencing are surprising even themselves as they become filled with information that they find more detailed, wording and tone that they have not previously had access to, and in some cases an entirely new feel to the energies surrounding them.

This reflects exactly what we have so often discussed for quite some time now. It reflects precisely the change in the energies surrounding them, and surrounding all of you. It also reflects the changes in your abilities to sense these energies, although they might be a bit more practiced than others in doing so. It reflects the ability of yourselves to contain more of the energy of your own Higher Selves, which we capitalize in order only to distinguish that of which we speak. For the purpose of illustration we speak of self and Self. And that does not seem odd to you, perhaps. But please realize that our goal, your goal, is the realization of no difference between the two.

And there, dear ones, we have just connected the dots. What you may have noticed in the evolution of the channeled messages is a reflection of the changes in the channelers and also in yourselves. Are you there yet? The answer will always be no. And the answer will also always be yes, you are more there today than ever before.

This is a journey, dear family. And you are flying along magnificently. As each of you learn a portion, remember a portion, feel a portion, so does it change each and all of you. And these changes radiate outwards into the all. As you continue to 'do the work', as you term it, we will continue to insure that you receive all of the support appropriate to where you are. That is our function, and as we have said, our joy.

* * * * * * * * * * *

We would speak today on the topic of clarity.

16

As you are more than well aware, whenever the communication between physical and non-physical is done in this manner, meaning telepathically, there is always some level of distortion. This is due to the necessity of using the faculties of the receiver. The mind of the receiver is involved, which brings into the process the experiences and beliefs, the emotions and fears, as well as the greater or lesser vocabulary and understanding of the channel as well.

Many of those whom we choose to employ in this fashion make great efforts to insure that they are as clear as possible when involved in this process. Many make it their goal to improve constantly. And we, too, do our part in both clearing their abilities to receive and in continually urging that they remain focused and intent on being always just a bit better. We do bring this message to you so that you may feel comfortable in what you read or hear whenever the message resonates with truth for you. But we have another reason for broaching this subject at this time.

You will have noticed, and perhaps experienced for yourself, the increase in the number of individuals whom we are now able to reach in this manner. That is to say, perhaps even you are beginning to sense the beginnings of contact with what you term 'the other side of the veil'. If that is the case, we urge you to take to heart the lines above.

In some cases, you may be so strongly influenced that it feels as if it is being thrust upon you, although you know, of course, that such is not the case at all. In some cases, it may be in response to your own conscious efforts. That is the most prevalent case. And there are many variations between those two.

We are urging you, whatever your personal experience, to maintain your intent to improve each day. Let us not forget to remind all of those receiving this in print or audio format that nothing is happening here which is not equally available to themselves, perhaps with some effort, but available nevertheless.

Should you choose this path, you have our assurance that your own 'team', your guides etc., will be more than willing to meet you halfway, so to speak. Be open to this in whatever way it manifests for you. We know that a great many of you who will read this are daily amused with what you call angel numbers, feathers on your paths, coins, etc. These are indeed synchronicities which you and your 'teams' have agreed upon as ways to get your attention and begin to communicate.

If you recognize this and intend to explore and widen the experience, you will discover ways to do so. That is the nature of the time and also of those who are reading this now. And let us not forget those who are listening to this now. We are, in a sense, drawing closer now, and it is time for you to know this. Enough for now. We may very well address this again later.

* * * * * * * * * * *

Let us discuss with you today the ways in which you interpret the channeled messages which you are given. We, of course, know that these will be received in the manner that they are. But it will be helpful, perhaps, for you to see the things that we see.

Many channels and their messages are influenced more than others by their own belief systems, by their pre-disposition toward one interpretation of information or another. This may be slight or it may not. All messages are, because of the methods involved, meaning telepathy, subject to greater or lesser degrees of accuracy. This is not to convey, nor is it meant to, any disapproval of anyone who is trying very hard to provide the best information they can to you in these times. Every sincere effort is appreciated.

In our description of this process, we have now arrived at the point where there is a readable or audible message for your access, exactly like what you are reading or hearing now. Each of you will read or hear this and will accept or reject it according to its resonance with what you already believe. And at this point, the message is further changed. You have a children's game, called Telephone, which illustrates this very process. In the game, the more people involved, the more the original message is changed.

Now, it is also possible for the message to be changed more toward its original intent. And here we come to the point we wish to make. If, once each individual receives the message, each of you take what you have heard or read, and sits with it in your heart, your heart will help you to get the most truth out of it that is possible for you in the moment. If you ask, you will have as much help with that as the channel did when he or she received it. This is the discernment of which we speak so often.

Your ability to do this is growing as we progress along this journey. Looking back, we are sure you can see how your understandings have been changing, sometimes gently and gradually, sometimes radically. We see some having what you call "Aha!" moments in which many pieces of a puzzle fall together. Aren't those wonderful?

One last thing we would mention. No one on your plane of Creation has the entire truth of anything. Therefore, we ask that you judge neither yourselves nor any other. After all, you can only compare their portion of the truth to your own portion.

Rather, it would serve you well to honor the other for being on a journey just as you are, and to wish them the very best. That does not mean you need to espouse anything with which you do not agree, does it? Simply honor their efforts at living and learning as best they can.

At this point, we would like to honor each of you for your living and learning as best you can, and also to offer our love and support in your doing so. You really are doing better than you realize.

ASCENSION

Here are the messages from 2013 that address the topic of our ascension. I am struck, as I read them, how everything that has happened in the past two years, at least to me, fits so well into what they describe.

We will speak with you today about the rising tide of which almost all of you who work with and for the light are becoming aware.

This is something which we have mentioned a while ago, but which, as it was not quite so obvious, even the most sensitive of you had to take on faith. Lately it has been growing day by day, and at such a rate that those who meditate or perhaps have a daily prayer practice, and even those who spend much time communing with your dear planet, are seeing, even feeling, unmistakably.

For those who have stayed the course, it is no longer a matter of wondering if something is happening or not. Even the most ardent of you had moments of that kind of thinking prior to now. As you move deeper and deeper into the uplifting energies, you will know beyond doubt that, at least for yourselves, ascension is indeed in progress. But know this also, brothers and sisters. The energy, which is producing such profound change in your own bodies, and here we mean to reference your physical, emotional, mental, and spiritual bodies, is also embracing each and every other being in its path. There is no escaping it.

Now, how an individual human may react to it is a matter of choice. That is true. But in the longer run, we promise you that far more will choose the high road than choose the low. There is still a bit of work left for you, is there not? But we suggest that the finding of, and healing of, the last little bits is becoming easier and easier. There are many, many lightworkers who are now more than prepared to help each other upon the way, enough we assure you, to take care of all those who will eventually begin to turn to you for aid.

Many times you have asked, "Why me? Why this? Why now?" You will begin to understand the extreme importance of the reminders of your lessons now. We say reminders because you have traveled this path for so long that there was really very little that you had left to learn when you took on this job. What was important, and you are accomplishing it amazingly well, was that you first clear up the huge amounts of fear, guilt, and feelings of little worth that you brought forward from other experiences. Some of you were already so clear that you actually had to borrow some of that from others. "Why would I do that?" you ask. Because you are such loving beings that you decided to have the experiences you would need to do the work that you knew would be needed here.

Yes, there is a lot left to do. But we think you will believe us now when we tell you that what you are to witness from this time forward will more than be worth the price of admission. And what is more important, what you are experiencing within eclipses even that. We see you striding forward in excitement and love, and we are very glad that each of you got their ticket for this ride.

* * * * * * * * * * *

One of the most read posts on my blog is a listing of many of the symptoms of rising kundalini energy in the body. It is the most read post over the last two years. In this message you will see some advice on how to deal with those things when you experience them.

Today we will speak about health and what you term ascension symptoms.

The energies which are being sent to your environment, and those which your planet is passing through, are causing minor discomforts in some, major discomforts in others, and still others, though few, are experiencing real pain.

Of course the differences can be attributed to several things. Firstly, what is the condition of the body, mind, and spirit of the subject? That is you. How freely are you giving yourselves to the transition? How rapidly has your Higher Self and your soul determined that you should make this change? And do not overlook the possibility that there may be conditions that can and should be treated by your medicine.

In many cases, however, your medicine cannot find or understand the conditions you are reporting. Pain and discomfort are signals, dear ones—either signals of the existence of a condition or of the existence of resistance. The easiest thing to try would be for you to truly fling yourselves into the future with all your hearts. So much for resistance.

But in many cases your bodies themselves are storing, unknown to you, fears, angers, resentments, resistances, and regrets from this life, prior lives, even those passed down to you in your DNA from those who came before you. "Well, how in the world am I to deal with that?" you ask. We shall give a few suggestions.

To begin with, know that the unconditional love that is enveloping you now will eventually overcome all of those resistances and you will ascend if you have decided to do so. That may be sooner or it may be later. And patience is much easier when one is comfortable, is it not?

You may decide to go it on your own and, through your meditations and prayers, seek out and solve the issues for yourselves. In this case, help is available through your connection to the Source of your being. But we suggest you not be like the one who insists he will be saved by the Almighty and ignores the rowboat that has been sent to save him from the flood.

Lastly, dear ones, there are a great many "new" healing methods that have become available to you during these last years that can deal with these kinds of things in ways the your medicine has never learned to do. We have put the word new in quotes because they are simply things that are now being remembered by yourselves. They address these things through your energetic and spiritual side.

Understand that when something is cleared for you on those levels, the effect must show up on your physical side. So if you are not wishing to live with the discomforts until they disappear on their own, then look for the type of healing that most resonates with your beliefs. We say that because, although it may not be the most powerful, it will be the one that your beliefs will allow to work for you. You can progress to another when you choose to.

Beliefs, you see, are things that you have constructed, knowingly or not, in order to protect you. And in many cases, they can actually be that which is causing you problems. They are very often not in agreement with what you think you believe in your conscious minds.

That may not sound possible to some of you, but we assure you it can be true. As an example, you may think that you trust your Creator with all your heart, but then ask yourself why you resist change or spend any time at all worrying about the future.

So the final thought we would give you today is this. Wherever you are, and whatever your situation is, there is, somewhere in your physical or spiritual environment, help available if you want it. You can find it if you look for it. You will need to accept it when you find it. Ask yourself if perhaps your opinions do not stand in the way. Or is it perhaps that you are proud of being a loner?

In any case, you are moving on. And the truth is, you are doing exactly what you need to do in this moment. That is because what you are doing will inevitably lead you eventually to where you have decided to go.

* * * * * * * * * *

We will speak now of some of the things you may expect in your continued process of ascension. The question has been posed to our channel, and thereby to us, "What of those who are mentally incapacitated, those in institutions, those who are elderly and refuse to listen?" And further, we have heard many times questions about children, parents, dogs, cats, and a long list of others. We ask you to please rework your understandings of what this process is.

Please release your ideas of transporting to some other dream world, in whatever fashion, and leaving others behind. Everything and everyone in this universe is being affected by the rising of, and expansion of consciousness. It is impossible to not be affected.

That being said, dear friends, every person, every animal, and every being is in its own place with its own past and its own future. Do you wish to choose that future for them? Even your Creator has allowed them to explore creation with their own free will. Would you imagine for yourselves greater wisdom than this?

You have, as a collective consciousness, chosen to slow down your ascent to bring all along on the journey. This is a journey of consciousness, dear hearts. And that decision, that marvelous decision that you all have made, is equivalent to something called the bodhisattva vow. But allow yourselves to understand that the light that is permeating your world at this moment is raising every cell, every molecule, every atom, and every particle in its path.

All are not duplicates of each other now, and they will not be in future either. If that were the goal, there would be no need for the infinite number of beings that make up the One. Now, since these concepts are a bit if a problem for you, since you continue to hang onto some of your limitations still, we would ask you to remember and focus on this one thought. You are each and all a part of that One, and as you raise yourselves, you raise the All.

That means that your ascension aids the ascension of each of those you asked about at the beginning of this message. You may not be able to convince them. In some cases, you may not even be able to communicate with them. But you are precisely the ones who can aid them in their growth, because you cannot not affect the All. Please, therefore, release worry and fear and teach yourselves to focus on your goal. Teach yourselves to build as clear a picture of what world you would have for yourselves and others.

Your input is valued, valuable, and powerful. You ARE the co-creators. Imagine, if you will, your Creator saying, "You Are the I AM that I AM." Imagine it because it is true. And then value yourselves accordingly. We do. And your Creator does, as well. Learn to refrain from thinking or speaking of yourselves or others in lesser terms. The one standing next to you and the one wearing your shoes are both amazing beings of the light.

DISCERNMENT

As always, we ask only that you weigh in your own hearts the value of the words as received. This is called discernment and is the only measure that you should apply.

Our aim is not to convince or cajole, but to offer the very best help we can to those who have taken on the most difficult of tasks. What you term ascension has never been easy. It has never been something one could expect to accomplish in one lifetime. And nowhere and never has it ever been done while wearing a physical body and continuing to do so afterward.

Even the progress you have made together so far is quite remarkable. If you feel, as an individual, that you are ready at his time to continue this amazing journey, we ask that you let go now of all that you know is anchoring you in your dramas and lower feelings. Reach with all your intention, acceptance, and joy for what you perceive as your highest best possible self. You are supported.

You are deeply immersed now in those energies of divine love that will make your success possible. All of those things that have held you back for thousands of years are being removed from your path. They cannot endure these frequencies. Realize, however, that this will not be done for you. The efforts of self-discovery and clearing must be made. The existence of others who are protecting and urging you forward is not the question any longer. But understand please, that your placing all of your hopes in having someone or

29

something swoop in to magically save you from yourselves is not in the game plan, as you call it. You wrote the plan, dear ones, and that is not it.

Now, if we may venture to give you a bit of good news, the progress being made on all fronts is continuing to accelerate. Individuals are awakening at a more and more rapid pace. Understanding is growing. The rise in the collective self-worth is wonderful. The determination to change your world for the better is growing and hardening. Changes are beginning to be seen in places thought impossible not weeks ago. True, it is only glimmers so far. But the light is advancing.

We will make no promises. We understand how they have seemed hollow to this point for many of you. We will simply say that all who watch are joyous and amazed at what you are doing. There is still some ways to go, however, so don't pause to pat yourselves on the back just yet. But do not become discouraged either. You are here because, of all who wished to undertake this task, you were the best hope. Reach inside and find that light within. Cherish it and use it for all it is worth. It will bring you home.

* * * * * * * * * * *

Our topic for this day will be the messages that we send to you and your trust in us. This is a very crucial question to the entire subject of ascension. It brings into sharp focus the need for you to have developed discernment that you can rely upon rather than allowing events about you or the words of others to sway you to and fro like a leaf in the wind.

We believe we have never asked for you to believe in, to trust, the messenger, but have always urged you to base your judgment upon the content of the message itself. Further, we will tell you now that messages that are sent to you from the higher dimensions, particularly those which contain the truth of the divine Creator, will always carry a detectable feeling to you which you will sense as a loving embrace. It is the transmission to you of that for which your hearts have yearned forever since you have journeyed away from it.

We do not appeal to your intellects, neither to any other emotion or feeling than that. You may home in on Divine Truth like a beacon by this energy of unconditional love. There still are among you, even among those of you with sincere intent, those who persist in trying to analyze and dissect this phenomenon. There are those who persist in asking for material proof. There are those who continue to ask when such will be given.

Dearest ones, you have been doing this since the time of Enoch, of Abraham, and before. And for all that time, and before, you have been taught that you, you physical co-creators of your own existence, are the ones who make those things happen. Yet you continue to look up into the starry sky and say, "When?" You wait for a savior. Well, your savior is standing in your shoes. And the time is now, if you so choose.

Sometimes what is needed is a little straight talk, is this not so? We know that many, many of you are indeed not in need of this today. You are far past that now. Yet there are also many who still need to hear this once again. Once again, the community that has been built is being battered by those who claim to know better than to believe or trust. And once again, we are telling you to trust your heart.

Go within, connect with your highest concept of the Divine, whatever name you call it by, and ask for assurance. We ask nothing further than this.

* * * * * * * * * * *

On this day we would speak further on the subject of discernment. This is a matter that is of great importance at this time. It has always been important, of course, but at this juncture, when so much of your future rides upon your state of being, your evolution in consciousness, it is more important than ever.

You will wish to do that which will spur you onward, and not that which will in any way delay your progress. The misguided wish to remain in the status quo is, however, still strong in some quarters, weakening yes, but still presenting problems for you wherever possible.

There is a flood of information available to your intellect that has reached proportions not known for many thousands of years to those on this planet. It is in your best interest to learn how you may best deal with it. How may you best decide what is of value to you and what is not? What is true and what is not? Who and what may you trust?

We could take you on a long drawn out discourse on angels, guides, ascended masters, and the creative beings. And all of that would apply, of course. But this will be a short message, dear ones, because the best answer is a very short one.

There is a very reliable and simple way in which all of those above mentioned, and let us not forget your own highest selves, communicate with you from moment to moment. Yes, we do communicate with you from moment to moment. And there are many and various ways that you may use to receive that communication, but that is not what is needed here. What you need is to be able to tell in an instant whether to accept what you are hearing, seeing, or reading, or not to accept it. And there is also the possibility of setting aside your acceptance or rejection until more evidence is available. Is there such a way?

We would tell you that there is. It is not something we have never told you before. It is, however, something that is so simple that you have not given it the consideration you should. Here, dear friends, is the key. When you are reading, watching, or listening to what is before you, be very aware of how it makes you feel in your heart. Your heart is very, very wise. It is that within you that is 'connected' at all times. This is the place in you in which 'the knowing' resides. It is the home of mind. We did not say intellect. It is where mind is connected to your earthly being.

Let us not get into a discussion of that today. Let us just say that your heart has waited patiently throughout your entire lifetime for you to begin to earnestly listen to what it can tell you. Let us also assure you that never, ever, will it mislead you. But the 'trick', if there is one, is that you need to listen. By that we mean do not discount, ignore, or reason away what you feel.

If you will learn to go through your day-to-day lives in this fashion, you will find yourselves quickly becoming happier and much less stressed. And sooner or later you will come to know from whence those feelings come. We are, as we have told you many times, with you in every moment. You are never, ever, alone. And you are loved unreservedly. This, as you say, you may take to the bank.

* * * * * * * * * * *

Your ability to discern truth is once again being awakened within you. This is not a new thing, but something that has been intentionally kept muted and unused. Even when it began to return you were distracted at every turn.

Yet you have managed to piece together an increasingly accurate picture of the true state of your world. To this point, however, even though great amounts of information have been uncovered, most of it has reached very limited audiences. Although your communication networks, what you call your Internet, have access to much, you are yet not putting together anything like a complete picture. You are still hampered by divisions among you. You still allow the tools of ridicule and misinformation to blind you to some of the truth. And you still are unable to consider that much of the most unnerving things could possibly be true.

This is very convenient for those who are hiding behind the screen that it affords. You are continuing to grow, and your awareness is punching holes in that screen now until it truly is most tattered. We hear many of you say, "Bring it on." Each of you now, please refrain from saying that, and quietly ask yourselves, "What is it that I may be refusing to see? We say this only to prepare you for what you will surely see shortly. And again, we assure you that, as great a shock as some of it will be to you, the freedom that will follow upon its heels will be even greater.

Look within now and find the peace that will allow you to stand steady and in loving strength as your world continues to change around you. Breathe light in. Breathe love and gratitude out. You are our brother and sister angels, our family, at work. You are deeply loved.

CHANGE

Our deepest love and appreciation for each and all of those who continue upon their paths is what we desire to begin this message with. Please be assured that no moment passes in which this is not foremost in our hearts.

The physical changes to your cellular makeup, in response to the continuing barrage of cosmic light, continue at a rapid pace, and the corresponding increase in your personal light is obvious to all those observing your world. Changes are increasing in your economic systems. Other changes are increasing, as well. But because the reports you have available do not come from the five major information conglomerates which spoon feed the world with lies and half-truths it is easy for many to deny all of this.

There will, of course, come a time when these things can no longer be denied. Because so many of you continue in your conviction and efforts toward personal change, this will occur sooner rather than later. But, as some of your governments have learned to their chagrin, imposing massive change from the outside never, ever works. Easing the path for the change to surface from within, however, will work. And it is to your everlasting credit that you have chosen to maintain your efforts until that can happen for as many of your brothers and sisters as possible.

Some of them will grumble. Some will accuse. Some will turn their back upon you. But you have not allowed that to deter you in the past and we know it will not stop you now. You have always found the strength to continue and ways to proceed. We have always given whatever aid and inspiration possible. These things will never change. There are lessons being learned on both sides of this question.

We understand that this is not what you most desire to hear at this point. You wish us to tell you that at such an appointed hour, on such an appointed day, your world will be transformed completely. Were there to be such an occurrence, dear hearts, it would be necessary for either separate worlds to exist, or your new world would begin to deteriorate due to the fact that billions of your co-creators would still be creating according to their state of consciousness, just as they are now. Yes, they would continue to evolve in their understanding, just as they are now. Yes, the outcome would eventuate in a completely ascended planet, just as it will now.

Most of you who read these messages understand what has happened and are having almost daily personal evidence that much has changed for them. Most understand that not only are you changing in your inner beings, but you are indeed being helped immensely by your spiritual guides and teachers. Some are indeed beginning to see evidence that change has occurred in their physical environment. There is plenty to cheer your hearts and motivate you, dear friends, if you look for it. And there will be much more surfacing as this monumental change continues.

We ask you to continue doing what you do. Resolve to re-double your own personal work to change yourselves. Find comfort, peace, and love within.

You have not lost anything, nor will you. In fact, we tell you that at the very least, your sense of community has been vastly enhanced. We would tell you that our love for you has increased, but that, dear ones, loving you more, is something that may be impossible. Breathe in the unconditional love and light from your Creator, find the peace it brings to you, and sit in that space until you are once again centered and strong.

* * * * * * * * * * *

Today we will focus upon the subject of changes to your world once again. If you are one who gains most of your information from the television or newspapers, then you may very likely have overlooked several hints pertaining to what we are about to tell you. If you also, or exclusively, get information from what has been termed alternate media, then perhaps you have begun to put together a slightly different picture of what is occurring at this time.

The hints of impending change are available for you to see, if you wish to see them. And, as we have told you on more than one occasion to expect, they are beginning to gather a momentum of their own. We have used the terms snowball and avalanche. Well, perhaps they have not reached quite those proportions yet, but they will. And we will have had something to do with the energies and nudges which have produced the climate in which this will happen.

But you, my dear friends, are the ones who will carry out these changes, the ones who will see them through. We suggest you begin to read and listen to what is happening around you with a new outlook. Begin to read beneath and behind what is being told to you. It will not be told to you in obvious terms just yet, although that will come soon enough.

We suggest, also, that you in the North American countries begin to look around beyond your borders, as much that you are not being told is happening elsewhere, and not enough weight is being given to its effect on your world yet.

There was a time when you determined the course of word events almost always. But there is a growing influence that is beginning to balance that out now, and it would be of benefit to understand that. There are immense changes afoot, dear ones. And, no, they are not of the fearful or catastrophic kind. Rather, your world is about to begin changing to be bountiful and beautiful for more than just a handful of its children.

If you can find just one thing to celebrate each day, you will both make yourself feel better and contribute to the progress you seek. Hold that good news in your heart, nurture it, and share it. The one other thing we would urge you to do is to look at what you desire from a situation, and not at what you do not. Be for something and not against something else. We think you understand that concept now.

* * * * * * * * * * *

Our topic for today is, once again, the accelerating change and your ability to perceive it. The change we are referring to is total. It is changing you internally, and this change is resulting in changes external to you, at least in your perception of internal and external, which is flawed to say the least. What you perceive as external change is a result of internal changes you have been able to make for yourselves due to the increased and increasing light which is available to you.

There is truly nothing external to you, and of course that is why you see changes around you, around your point of perception, and you understand, or misunderstand, that of course you had nothing to do with what you see because you further perceive yourself and other. This is more of the illusion. There is self, yes. But there is no other.

Enough of the riddles, you say? We agree, for now. You will understand things of this sort in your own divine timing. The point of this little exercise is to get you to stop looking around and thinking that nothing is changing. Dear ones, everything is changing. It always has. It always will. As has been observed before by your sages, if there is one constant in your universe, it is change. The question is, why do you not see the changes you desire? Is that not so?

You think such changes are not there to be seen? Well, they most certainly are, and they are increasing every day. If you truly desire to see them, and if you truly look for them, you will not miss them. But if you hold the cloak of denial about yourself, which is a way to protect yourself from disappointment, you will not see them. And as long as you hold onto that protection, that blanket, moth-eaten and musty though it is, you will not see them.

Things are moving along quite nicely now. We invite you to drop the blanket and look around. Things are not nearly as frightful once you make the decision to expect and look for the positive that is around you. Even the apparent bad news, such as peaceful demonstrations being repressed, can be seen for the positive influences they are when you change your own perspective.

You are, in fact, well into a period of immense and positive growth in awareness and consciousness. Millions of you are aware of the changes happening in yourselves. It can be time now for you to open your hearts and see the resulting changes in your world, but that is a decision you must make for yourselves. The strength to do so is now available to you. It resides in your heart. We keep saying that. We will continue to say it. Your entire new world resides in your hearts. In your own words, dear ones, go for it! Be the angels of peace, love, and change you came here to be.

* * * * * * * * * * *

We greet you today with news that your world, at least the world of those not in denial, is changing. Look more closely around you than the national and international news. Many of you stopped following that some time ago anyway. Look for the changing attitudes of those in your own communities. Look even at the opportunities being brought forward by those courageous enough to challenge the long prevailing attitudes that you want changed.

In the short run, not every one of these changes may manifest. In the long run, dear hearts, they all will. It all serves to awaken those who hear of it just that much more.

Look to what you call your social media. How rapidly are the attitudes and understandings changing there? Yes, even in spite of those who refuse to acknowledge it, and in spite of those who are paid to undermine it. Some still think, you see, that they have the power to influence what you think, but we assure you that the power to influence what you think is only yours, if that is what you determine. We say that because, in addition to your own power, you have called upon and activated ours. They are trying to put their fingers into the dike, as your story goes, but they are finding that they only have ten fingers and the dike is leaking in innumerable places.

Love is breaking out. Peace and freedom will surely follow. For those who continue to insist that nothing is happening, we have this response. You are wrong. Sorry, but you are wrong. The inner changes of millions of people are indeed happening now. And that, my friends, is what your societies and your world are made up of. It is all a reflection of you. And you are in the driver's seat now.

If you hope, you are powerful. If you believe, you are more powerful. If you see, hear, feel, know, and love, you are the most powerful of all. Join together now and show yourselves just what you can do in peace and love. Be your new world and then watch it appear before your eyes. It is who you are. It is why you are here.

* * * * * * * * * * *

What wonderfully complex creatures you are, able to say that things are not progressing as rapidly as you would like, and yet thinking that you have no time to finish everything. No wonder you amuse even yourselves at times. Let us look at things from another perspective, shall we?

There are changes occurring in every particle of creation at this time. There is no being, micro, macro, or cosmic, from your point of view, which is not being affected. Every atom you can perceive, every life form upon your earth, and every planet in your system are undergoing great change. Your scientists are quite aware of this, even though they are not telling you. Some are afraid, some are just confused. They have never seen, and do not understand, what they are seeing now. Some others think they know, but we would hasten to tell them that they do not.

There is relatively instantaneous change, evolution, ascension, afoot. But you, dear friends, being the complex beings that you are, and being able to invent things like increments of time, are able to view this so minutely that you can decry a lack of change. Well, my friends, let me tell you that, if there is one constant in your universe, it is change. You simply cannot live in a single moment that is like any other moment ever was or ever will be again. So basically all you are saying is, "I am unhappy with the state of things as I perceive them to be. I want more for myself. Are we there yet?" And our answer could be, "As long as you continue to hang on to your precious viewpoints, you will not see the changes you want." But we do not say that.

We do not say that because each atom, molecule and cell in your bodies is undergoing the same changes as all the others we spoke of. You are going to have the world you dream of, even though you seem to be dragging your way there.

Many of those who follow these and other messages are aware of, do feel, and are enjoying much personal change. As we have spoken before, this is what is driving things on your planet. Why? Because on your planet mankind is the driving force. As an aside, you have been driving in the wrong direction. And mankind is something that only exists as a collection of individuals. In other words, you determine what is happening. So complaining about the state of things will not get you where you wish to be. And yet you see us seemingly celebrating your advances.

Well, dear ones, look around. Look past your preconceptions. You are moving. Things are changing. And your inner as well as your outer worlds are becoming much improved. Love and blessings to those who are experiencing this firsthand. And even more love and blessings to those who have not begun to experience it yet. Truly it is time to begin to look to yourselves.

Our promise is this, if you will begin to look into your hearts, if you begin to ask daily for the changes in you that we discuss, you will find them. You are not undeserving. You are not unworthy. You are not to be left behind. Just present your I-am-a-child-of-Creator ticket and climb on board. You will be welcomed with open arms. In that moment, the answer to your question, are we there yet, will change from 'no' to 'yes'.

And to those already on this ride, let us say that you would be amazed to see how many others are finding the light every day

* * * * * * * * * * *

Today we will speak once more for a while about the continuing rise of important events on your planet. There is a growing flood of changes, both seen and unseen, which are changing your entire civilizations in ways that even those involved cannot see the scope of. Perhaps the only way to even begin to fathom the trends involved would be to detach oneself and try to reach a perspective removed from the fray, so to speak.

There actually is no facet of your existence which is untouched. Why is this? It is because every facet of your existence is created by your own collective consciousness. It is because you have determined it to be thus. It is because you, as stated many times before, are the co-creators of this world.

It is time for you to understand this in far deeper ways than ever before. As your acceptance of the responsibility of this grows, so will grow your power to use it. You have ensured that you would not assume this power in its fullest until you learned to accept the responsibility. You are far wiser in your wholeness than you know.

So many of you yet feel small, feel insignificant; even feel you are powerless to do anything. That must and is coming to an end now. You are becoming more and more aware of the larger being that you truly are, and as this happens, your greater Selves are more able to communicate with you and act through you. After all, they are you. It is desirable for you to look for these things, these inner changes, to want them, to accept them, and to reply with gratitude and the intent to exercise your highest abilities for the highest good. As has been said, if the only prayer you ever uttered were "thank you". It would be enough.

Divine energies such as have never before been available to you are now surrounding your planet, indeed your star system, in ever increasing purity and are influencing every being on your planet. Even if you do net yet feel the truth of that, prepare yourself to be amazed. Prepare yourself to live in joy and freedom. Better, decide to live that way. We are the ultimate conspiracy theorists. When you make that your decision, the universe will conspire to make it your reality.

* * * * * * * * * *

On this first day of your new month, in the midst of the greatly enhanced energetic flow to your earth which is being further heightened by the rare alignments in the heavens, you are once again allowing yourselves to expect almost instantaneous deliverance into an entirely new existence. And because most of you will not find millions in your bank accounts, new cars in your driveways, nor hear announcements of this or that on your televisions, will you once again cry foul?

Because you are told that there are certain changes in the future, and that change is certain in the future, you then set yourselves up for immense disappointment by imagining calendar deadlines into being. You have prior and recent experience of the results of this. Yet you continue to allow yourselves to get caught up in this kind of thinking. And the cry of "See? Nothing happened!" will rise again. And many more disillusioned hearts will fall away. And those who promised you this or that will find ways of deflecting the blame back onto you.

The truth is that huge change to what is invariably means huge resistance and huge obstacles. And you certainly cannot be blamed for wanting to see the light at the end of the tunnel.

This can all be avoided, as you really do understand by now, by not allowing the calendar to enter into the picture. There are huge and delightful things on their way into your reality. This has been revealed to you, and it is true. This is not going to happen in an instant because those of us on our side of the 'veil' snap our fingers and produce it for you. You have been told that you are the instruments of change, and that is also true. And even on the days when the most amazing changes begin to see the light, most of you will not see any change in your immediate existence. Your bank balance will not change. The media will not reverse itself and begin trumpeting the great news far and wide. And your day-to-day lives will change much more gradually than you imagine. Think about this. You know this. This is reasonable.

It is true that you have waited for a long time for these things to occur. It is understandable that you wish them to appear overnight. And in retrospect, that will be exactly how it will seem. But you have all had enough experience of life to know that it never seems that way while you are looking forward.

You **are** sitting in the midst of a time of immense change. You are. It is being driven by you, by your dreams, by your intent, and, yes, to a great extent, by your expectations. Strengthen those. Expect miracles. And also, dearest ones, although it may seem contradictory, look reality in the eye. See it for what it is.

What it is, is the things which you are changing, as well as the cause for your motivation. You, each of you, are the force which has come here to re-create this world. Do not allow the seeming lack of what you have dreamed to derail you. Hoard those dreams until the moment after you see them before your eyes. Celebrate that moment. Then move on, dear hearts.

You know life well enough by now to realize that by that time you will have even more dreams. This is how the universe operates. This is the work you do, unless this is the game you play. You can look at it that way, as well. But, even if all of the things you expect to happen occur on the same day, even if you do see huge miraculous things happening around you, it will not be the finish line. The race will not be over. There is no finish line, you see. There never will be. You will always want more. You will always want better. You will always be looking into the future for it. It is how you exercise your power. You are learning to do that in the highest and best way possible.

You are amazing. You are loved. You are respected. Give some of that love and respect to yourselves.

* * * * * * * * * *

We continue our discussion of good news.

It is our perception that many more of you are seeing the increase of more positive signs that are becoming more evident in the news you are reading and hearing. It is almost impossible to shut off all news, and we know that. But that is OK, because you will now begin to receive increasingly hopeful information. And you will continue to increase your abilities to receive from us possible positive twists to the story which are not so evident, as well.

This message will be short and to the point. It has been stated before in lengthier form. Perhaps a simple statement will make it clearer.

The Divine has decreed the end of this situation in which you have been mired for such a long time. The result of that is that ALL change will result in movement toward that end, no matter its intent, and no matter its appearance. So look behind the appearances, my dear family, and rejoice when you perceive what lies there.

Focus on the outcome you desire for ALL beings. We stand alongside you now and urge you to hold fast to your dream.

* * * * * * * * * * *

Dear friends, we meet you today in a period of integration and consolidation for you, a time for you to assimilate what you have gained thus far on your journeys. This will not be of great duration, and some of you may wish that it would last longer than it will. But there is still a long way to travel, even for the marvelous beings you are and continue to become.

Most of what we speak of now is still somewhat beyond your understanding. Still, we know that many of you are beginning to get the beginnings of such. You are seeing more of the light, more of who you are, more of where you are going.

For those of you who do not yet see, let us say that if this is the kind of message you follow, if this is the kind of dream that you hold in your heart, then you are most definitely upon this path as well. And let us also assure you that you are much further along than you now perceive. Looking about you, you may wonder how we can state such a thing. How can you possibly believe it?

Let us remind you of one or two things. Firstly, your desire and prayer are very definitely the fuels which impart your forward motion. And your intent provides the direction. And then, we remind you that you are a part of the oneness of the collective heart of humanity. You rise together. And it is a most beautiful and fantastic thing to see.

Know that each time you give your love, your best hopes, a hug, even a smile to another, each time you help them to feel better, it raises their state of being, raises your own, and raises the all. Each time you spend quiet time in your hearts in prayer, in meditation, or simply imagining the future you wish for your world, you bring it closer to you.

Very quickly now you will be once again thrust into the increasing flow of change, and the momentum and velocity of change will increase greatly. We have told you of this before. You have been patient. And you have, as a result of your intentions and prayers, and the purposes for which you came here at this time, made great strides in your inner selves.

Now the outer mirrors of that are going to reflect back to you an increasingly accurate picture of who you truly are. Your combined energy is beginning to be felt. Remember if at times things seem unsettled, and you do not see the positive direction they are heading, to simply know that your best interests are always our intent, and renew your own resolve.

These knowings, these intentions, these feelings are what power the change you desire. And know that you have our own intention and the energy of our love joined with yours at all times. Be not dismayed by anything that happens around you. Everything is happening now exactly as it needs to happen to bring about the very highest and best result of your collective vision, even though it may be impossible for you to see that from your perspective. Connect with us at any time that you need to renew your knowledge of that. We love you dearly are here for just that purpose, dear ones.

GREATER SELVES

We would like to discuss today a change which quite a few of you have begun to take note of, and we will use yourself and a few of those you have conversed with as an example. It is a phenomenon which has been around literally forever, but never have so many been in a position to notice or take advantage of it. Now, as you continue to raise your energy levels and frequencies, almost all of you are in a position to do so if you desire and intend to do so. You may also, stumble upon it, quite by accident.

Of course there are no accidents. So if this seems familiar to you, and it seems an accident, be aware that your Higher Selves and your guides have been moving you along your desired path, even though you seem blissfully unaware in your day-to-day consciousness. This, of course, is why you might wish to get deeper in touch with your Selves, in the higher sense. Nothing we tell you is beyond what you know in your hearts.

As we stated in the beginning, several of you have noted between yourselves that you have made decisions, or entertained ideas, and suddenly it seems your lives have taken off like a whirlwind, where before they were seeming so very placid, even stuck. You like to use that word, stuck.

You may be processing, you may be searching, or learning, or any of several other things. BUT, dear hearts, you are never stuck. You may be retreating, but you are never stuck. You may not be in touch with what is going on inside yourselves, but you are never stuck.

Go inside and learn what it is you are about. We cannot, and apparently have not, stressed this enough. But our point today is that when you spot the next step on this journey and summon the courage to take it, even though you do not see how it could possibly lead you anywhere successfully, be prepared to learn the power and wisdom of yourselves and your group of mentors, guides, and angels. Be prepared to have your lives take off like one of your rocket ships. And, my friends, you will not have time for the customary countdown. Do not let this arouse any fear of what we are saying. We tell you that it will bring you a feeling of joy such as you have seldom known. It will mean that you are well and truly on point with the purpose you came here for.

Blessed and divine beings that you are, it is time, more than time, for you to find out who you are.

* * * * * * * * * *

We wish now to discuss with you the expanding awareness of Self. You will note that we have written that with a capital S. We do not wish you understand that we are referring to the parts of yourselves which are currently conscious for most of you. And we say most of you because your state of awareness varies widely from individual to individual.

What is consistent, however, is that all of you, from the most conscious to the least, are receiving an empowering light from your Creator which is causing an expansion of that awareness. The more aware of you are receiving this and its resultant growth with gratitude and appreciation. This is causing you to evolve in ever more wonderful ways and is actually speeding the process for you. Others, being more determined to remain as they are, which is an impossibility by the way, are not understanding at all what is happening and are at a loss as to how to deal with what they are feeling. Quite a bit of the 'acting out', as you term it, is a result of this. Again we counsel you to offer whatever is asked for, but not to feel responsible for healing the entire populace. Those who choose not to see have free will also.

You will see also some very remarkable turn-arounds in those about you as and if they allow themselves to get a glimpse of what their alternatives are. It is not in anyone's nature to choose pain over gain, so you need not worry yourselves, even though you may not see at this time how their particular turn-around might occur. You are not aware of all they have seen and heard, nor are you aware of their inner responses. All will be as it should be.

Dedicate yourselves to the continuing expansion and upliftment of yourselves. That is what you are here to do, and that is the way in which you may most help the world and every sentient creature upon it. No, you do not fully appreciate that fact, as yet. But when you have reached the awareness we speak of, you will understand it.

Your responsibility to your Self is your responsibility to All. Of course, as you reach ever upward, you find yourselves sharing more and more with everything around you. You just don't see yet that the sharing continues out into the infinite. We assure you that it does. And the overall weight, the power, of what you are creating is soon to result in a world beyond your fondest dreams.

Be ever more deeply and constantly in your hearts now, dear ones, dear angels.

* * * * * * * * * * *

May we begin today by asking that all those who follow these messages hold only love and the intention for the highest and best outcomes when you observe what is going on around you at this time? Those highest outcomes will be, dear ones. But they will manifest sooner, and you will be far less affected by any negativity, if you guard yourselves against the thoughts and emotions that can invade your thoughts all too easily in these circumstances.

When situations and the actions of others which seem dubious, to say the least, come to your attention, remember that everything is part of a very complex flow of change which is designed both to bring your world into alignment with the highest good for all, and to show the futility of the last of the duality as the final lessons are learned.

We see that in your minds there is a picture of going to bed in a darker world and waking into a perfect one. And here is a paradox for you to contemplate. On the one hand, this will not happen in that way. It may happen that way for you individually, but there are billions of you in billions of unique states of awareness. And each begins from where he or she stands. On the other hand, it will, and has already happened in just that way. And we are, of course, viewing it in the context, and from the perspective of, what you call 'now time'.

Returning to the individual we were speaking of, and that would include each of you, we would have you feel the truth of this next image, if you will. You have, many of you reading this, reached the point in your personal changes, your evolutions, where you can now easily observe, easily feel, that you are well connected with parts of yourselves which not long ago you were unaware of. You feel connected to your Higher Selves, your oneness with All. This will be an ongoing process, an eternal process. But know in your hearts, dearest ones, that you are now on that path and will not fall from it again.

There is far more to this than you could possibly take in yet, but that too will change. One thing, and one thing only, need be uppermost for you from now on. Learn, discover, seek out, define, live, and BE love. All else will fall into place.

There are, as yet, viewpoints on your world from which such lofty scenes cannot be seen. They will fall away. And they will fall away due to what you have done, what you have become. In humble gratitude, learn to own that truth. It is all of you that have done it. But again in paradox, be proud of yourselves for the doing of it.

* * * * * * * * * *

We are here today to speak with you of the marvelous portal into which you are passing at this time. We would pass on to you some reminders of how to best utilize this wondrous opportunity, as there are still many of you who have not yet activated or remembered the wisdom which has been made available to you both recently and in your past.

Before stating that you have not such knowledge and wisdom, we would advise that you search inside with great intent and determination to find what is there, that you find that which is what you are, and not listen to the voice which tells you that it does not exist.

Feel that which is what you are. Feel all of what you are. Of course, that will be the quest of your forevers, but you can begin it or continue it today.

The time has come that will find you more able to see, to sense, to feel your Greater Selves than ever before. You will be able to learn, to remember, to expand, to grow, and to change in vastly more wonderful ways and in less time than ever before. You will find, if you look for it, a self that will surround you with all of the love that you ever need.

Perhaps you might want to begin by loving that self, by welcoming that self. We tell you that this part of you, or rather the all of you that you are a part of, will arrive bringing gifts you cannot yet even imagine. You may also wish to begin by holding gratitude for those gifts even before you open the package.

You are the ones chosen to bring to this world the things necessary for her, for society's evolution back into its intended purpose and condition. You were chosen to bring them and you have done so. It is time now for you to open the packages you have brought.

Some of you will now find abilities and talents unknown or long dormant. Some of you will think you have not such things to bring. Be assured that is not the case. Some, indeed much, of what is most needed is the simplicity, the purity, of your hearts. Do not underestimate the power of your love, of your compassion. Do not undervalue the effect of your smiles, of the hugs you give to those around you.

You cannot see with your physical eyes the extent of the change those seemingly small things bring to your world and beyond, but see in your imagination the possibility of it, and you may begin to understand. This is the time when those things are needed. This is the time when they will be needed more than ever before. Stay grounded. Stay centered. Stay focused. And maintain your steadfast intent to build the world that is a wondrous garden for all to play in.

HEART SPACE

Our message today is about allowing your minds to expand into areas which are perhaps new or perhaps long left unexplored. For quite some time now, you have allowed us to focus your awareness upon certain goals, and you have done very well. Now you have reached a sort of plateau, a place to gather yourselves and orient yourselves toward your purposes.

Take stock of your deep desires, both those current and those you felt far back in your memory, those you had given up on. Choose those which make your heart light and happy. Do not place any importance upon the opinions of others. When you are in your heart space, they are not there with you. Impossibility is not there either.

As big as your heart space is, it still will only hold you and those who can help build your lives of pure joy and abundance. This is the place to be true to who you really are. This is the place where we would like you to place your workbench. Look around you now. Notice that there are a great many new and shiny tools that you never had before. See the brand new boxes and containers of supplies. Open them and see the brilliant light reflect off of the contents. Now you are prepared to build whatever your heart desires. From now on, you may, and we wish you to, come back here as often as you like.

Come here and let your imagination flow. Remember to always use plenty of love in your creations, and perhaps even a little more than you think they will need, after all, you have as much as you can ever use. It is in the biggest chest of all, over in that corner, next to the case of intention. And always, always remember, no matter what is going on in your outside world, the real creation is here.

Whatever you see outside is a creation of the past. We don't think you want to live in the past. Come back here to create your future. Some of you will say to yourselves, "That is cute. I may try that." Some of you will recognize that it is Truth. Make it your Truth.

It is time now to begin creating this new world you have dreamed of for so long. But that creation needs to have the input of each of you. Lofty dreams are good, of course. But your personal lives are going to be a very integral part of what manifests from this point forward, and they are the pieces of the puzzle which you have the most control over. But let this not be business as usual from now on. You are the creators. Create what you love with joy.

We leave you to consider this until next we speak.

* * * * * * * * * * *

It is now obvious to those who are awakening that there have been great changes made by the rising energies within this last month, so much so that many are not only noticing the changes within themselves and each other, but are communicating this. There are, for some, even glimmerings of psychic openings where none were before. Almost all of you in this awakening state are feeling yourselves primed and ready for you know not what.

Our message to you today is that you do know what. It is the manifestation of your heart's deepest urgings. There has always been a time for this to happen. That time is now. The conditions in which you find yourselves at this point are best described as release. You are being released. What do you do now?

We suggest that your hearts and your highest selves know the answer to that and are much better prepared to handle it than you are. They have worked long and diligently getting you to this point, answering each intent and desire in your heart. So what we would recommend for those who have done their clearing and learned to spend time in their heart space is, throw the reins up onto the neck of your horse and hang on. Release.

Do today what is given you to do today. You need only concern yourselves with staying in alignment, keeping your state of joy and love alive. There is no reason to worry; no gain comes of it. Only keep your focus on that which brings you joy. Your Creator, your Higher Selves and your angels need only your request that they steer the ship. Once you have been able to do that, you will find it much easier to spend time sharing the love and peace you find within with all others. And that, dear ones, is the place to be. But if you are in constant struggle to answer your own needs and wants, it is very difficult to truly devote yourself to others, is that not true?

Yes, you can make an effort to do so, but you always find yourself falling back. Find the place of knowing that you are worthy, loved, and provided for. Then you will find that your heart readily begins to wish the same for all other beings.

We understand that a very great number of you have understood much of what we are saying now for a while, but those to whom that applies will please understand that there are now numbers awakening for whom these concepts are just being discovered. There are still more than a few who consider themselves lightworkers who struggle daily with the same old problems. Let us, we on this side and you on that, help them free themselves from those old situations and feel the freedom of this new energy, this new world. Their contributions are going to be needed as we move ahead now.

* * * * * * * * * * *

We speak over and over about your hearts. Let us begin today's message with that and see a little of why it is so important.

You have all been told, for as long as you can remember, that you think with your brain. Actually you do not. Your brain is a marvelous instrument, but it is only an instrument. You are more than a little likely, as you are one who reads these messages, to understand that you are not a package of meat and bones with a life, a mind, and a soul, but a life, a mind, and a soul that lives in a package of meat and bones. You temporarily inhabit your body, and for the time that such is the case, it is actually within you, even though it feels as if you are within it.

The connecting link between you, as a life, and your temporary home, is another one of your bodies which contains centers of energy which perform certain functions for you. Of these centers, your teachings have given major importance to seven. And of these seven, one happens to be located in the vicinity of the organ that pumps blood through your systems. It is this we refer to when we say your heart.

As applies to your life, it is this center which is associated with the feelings of love, compassion, and those higher feelings that we speak so often about. Other major centers are devoted to other things. For instance, feelings dealing with survival are centered lower down in the system. And the feelings we call higher, the love, compassion, empathy, and so on, are felt most strongly through this heart center. Now there is nothing that is a part of you which is not important, so higher, as we just used the word, does not mean that other feelings are not necessary or important. The urge to run when startled is hardly less important, do you see? But the ability to identify with the suffering of another, to love all life, and to desire with all one's heart to attain spiritual goals is rather lofty, is it not? What you have often missed is that these things are not only not possible, but not desirable, when life is hanging on a thread. So the word higher needs to be understood a little differently.

But since you have a computer connection, and are probably reading this or listening to it after it has been translated and recorded, we will assume that such is not the case for you. Therefore, you have the luxury of time and resources to spend time considering these higher feelings. All we can say about that is, "Good! You are not wasting the opportunity." That makes a point, but it was always understood that you would not, once you found yourself where you are, devote yourself to anything else.

Now... your heart. This is the place where dwells the you that we communicate with. When your heart is open for business, you are well upon this proverbial path that you love so much to speak of. And the feelings that will begin being felt very, very strongly by you when you have your attention in this place, this heart, are the messages which come directly from your Creator, from us, from your Higher Selves, your guides, and others who love you more than you could possibly understand yet. We who speak with you here, in this you have called your inner temple, have no other purpose than to lift you up into the very best and highest you can possibly be.

This is why, dear ones, we speak incessantly of your hearts. If all of that gives you some small understanding of why we wish you to spend time each day in quietude, within your heart space, then this was a well spent discussion. Communication with you is, you see, what we are all about. Angels are called messengers, but messengers from whom and to whom? You, dearest ones, are the reason for our being here. We love you.

* * * * * * * * * * *

As you can see, things are beginning to break loose now. They will continue to pick up steam and, as we have told you for quite some time, will become quick enough to have you in a state of disbelief.

There will be people all around you who are unable to process what they are seeing and who will retreat into total denial. You need not spend your energies convincing anyone of anything, dear ones. Events and truth will take care of that. But understand that they will be in dire need of ears who listen, if not agree, as their seemingly entire worlds fall to pieces around them. Be not smug in your knowing. Find in yourself any tendencies to even think or feel "I told you so."

Compassion for those who are cut loose from their moorings is what will be most needed now. Millions have known only what they have been spoon-fed all their lives. They have been told that lies are truth and truths were lies. They will be hurt. They will be angry. They will want to vent their anger and frustration. Be there for them.

When they have calmed down somewhat, they will have questions. Even then, the wisest course will be to answer the questions and let them proceed at their own pace to the next question. There is no need to lecture or teach. Events will take care of that soon enough. Very quickly millions of doubters will become seekers.

At this time, while things are still in the simmering stage, continue to seek yourselves. Ah... we like that. Continue to seek your Selves. You will need that connection as never before, but also, you have never had so great an opportunity to create that connection.

If you still do not have a regular daily practice of meditation, we urge you to establish one. Learn to center yourself. Learn to ground yourself. Learn to spend time in your heart space. Find your Source, your Creator, your I AM. You need no one else to do that, dear friends. You need only your own sincere intent and effort. We promise you that you will be met with open arms long before you get halfway. Find the peace in which your true heart resides. It will be important to you.

Seek the possible best outcome in every new turn of events now and watch as your prayers come to fruition.

IMAGINATION

Our purpose today will be to point out to many of you the tools which you have in your personal workshops, and which you do not recognize, understand, or give credence to due to the conditioning of your environments and societies. It is important now for you to find and begin to utilize these to the fullest extent possible for you.

Of course your workshop, if you remember, is located in the heart space you find with intent when you close your eyes and move your focus into your heart. There is more to this which you may find and which we may discuss in a later message.

The first and most important tool is your imagination. We think the most detrimental phrase in this regard is, "That is just your imagination." Well, we suppose a worse one is, "It is only my imagination." Your imagination is the language in which your spirit speaks to you. It is the tool by which we can speak to you. Great booming voices are not likely to begin coming from the heavens for you. You must not only begin to give credence to the things which appear in your imaginations, but rejoice that you have such a wonderful tool at your disposal. Try for the exultant feeling of, "What a wonderful thing I have imagined!" Imagine that! We tease you.

Now, let's refine that just a bit. If something comes up unbidden, undirected, into your mind, then some part of consciousness is communicating with you. That is hearing, seeing, or whatever other description you wish to give your perception. "But I don't see anything" is not understanding the process. Yes, some of you are what is termed clairvoyant, but that is not what we are talking about. Perhaps it is better if you learn to think in terms of perceiving, not seeing or hearing.

There is also the imagination that you produce with intention. This is visualization. This, my dear ones, is also known as prayer. It is the most powerful form of prayer. If you can understand this and imbue this with feelings, you will have a most powerful tool indeed. Then if you can learn to add, in your imaginations, smells, sounds, colors, etc., etc., then you will have something really powerful. These prayers are not learned or memorized. They originate in your heart. We always return to your heart.

The final thing we would say is this. In your hearts, you have emotions and you have feelings. You may not understand at first what we mean by that. But you will come to realize that feelings are the language of your very soul. When you are able to discern those, you will have found your most reliable guidance system of all.

Enough for today, my brothers and sisters. We see you walking in amazement through the new world you are discovering. Wonderful!

* * * * * * * * * * *

Our message today will be, as always, one of encouragement in tumultuous times.

What you see around you can only seem to be chaotic as you can see only the merest glimpse of anything other than the breakdown of the old wherever you look. The final result can, so far, only be seen in your imagination. This requires what you term a leap of faith.

So be it then. Leap! Leap with gusto. Leap in joy. Leap toward the most wonderful and abundant world you can imagine. That process is what has built and is building the world you want to live in. Spend all the time there that you can. Be the daydreaming person you were when you were enjoying your summer days as a child. Allow yourself now, however, to do it with purpose.

What are your own particular fondest dreams? There are many millions of you in this process. You do not need to imagine it all. Just imagine what, as you term it, 'rings your bell'. After all, that is why you are there. There are many others there to ring the other bells. If you like, and if you can, imagine the magnificent chorus of all the bells.

Also, for those of you who are feeling energy running through you at times, we have a suggestion of something you may wish to try. We think you will like the result. When you do feel those energies surrounding and flowing through you, realize that they are unconditional love... and return it. Allow the inflow and the outflow to feed upon each other. There will be no need for you to imagine the result.

LIGHT AND ENERGY

Our message for today will be simple and to the point. We are always speaking to you about energy, love, and light. That is the primary focus of this channel and will remain so for a time. Just as a coach of one of your sports teams will continually drill his team on basics, basics, basics, so do we wish to remind you over and over again of certain things. The most important of these is your connection to Creator's love.

When we speak of light or energy, we are speaking of the same thing. Please understand that you are always connected to this light, this love. Without it you would not be, would not exist. It is the very essence of yourselves. However, as readers of these messages, we assume that just existing is not your primary goal. Therefore, we are always bringing to your attention things which you may do to enhance your progress along your chosen paths.

There are a great many things which will help you along your way: visualizations, meditations, actions, attitudes, etc., etc. All of these may be very helpful at times. Your connection to your Creator's love and light, however, is the basic thing we would like to stress. This is something which will always, always see you through. It will always be healing. It will always provide you with what you need. In fact, it is more likely to know what you need than you are yourself.

Have you ever wished for, prayed for, even thought of something without it being known to Source? Of course not. What we are saying is, your first

73

and foremost priority should be to establish your intentional and conscious connection to Creator and maintain it jealously each and every day. At first, you may begin by imagining the light, love, and energy pouring into you. But quickly you will find that you begin to feel a response that does not depend upon your imagination. At that point there are many things you might think, imagine, pray, or intend. All of those are alright. None of them are necessary. You only need to bring into yourself, and therefore your entire field of being, more light, more love. Always more light, more love. Any doubt? More love. Uncertainty? More love. Fear? Worry? More love. Illness? More love.

This is something we see you forgetting at times when you encounter bumps in your path. We therefore stress it as the most basic thing. Open yourselves and allow it to happen and you will always find what your heart needs. You will also notice that we include no warning of side effects or of overdose. It is even alright if you are nursing or pregnant. Well, we thought to lighten this up a bit.

Remember, all the light you want, all the time, and then more.

* * * * * * * * * *

Today we will speak once again of energy, but we will limit ourselves to discussing those energies which have been building for quite a long time around your earth to influence all willing beings upon their paths to ascension. You know them, you feel them, and by now many of you have learned to invite and use them to their highest potential.

We speak of energies, and varying types and frequencies of energy are indeed present, but in truth all energy is at its base the pure and unconditional love of Creator. Further, all is One. It is to bring you to higher and higher realizations of this most basic truth that this flood of energy in such high concentrations is being brought to you. To be more accurate, you are being brought into ever-higher concentrations of it. And as the energy signature of your planet and all upon her rise, you are attracted to even higher states. Imagine a graphic curve which has traveled fairly steadily, begun to rise at an ever sharper rate, and has now headed almost straight up. If that were a plot of your resources would it not bring a smile to your face? Well, that is exactly what it has the potential to be. It will be eventually that for each of you, dear friends, but we will give you once again a couple of nudges to help you bring that to be a bit more rapidly accomplished for you.

We remind you that you may invite and accept this into yourselves. You may express your gratitude for what it brings you, seen or not. You may give thanks for who and what you are and are becoming. All of these things will make this much easier for you and speed the process along. Dwelling on any discomforts along the way will unfortunately have the opposite effect. But perhaps it is time to speak about a few other things of which you should be aware.

Many of you see others skipping happily along this path and wonder why you don't appear to be moving at all. May we offer you now some possibilities to examine?

Let us consider the easiest one first. You may have a contract to fulfill. There may be an agreement between yourself and another to help one or both of you to accomplish something in this lifetime which is not yet finished. Quite often these contracts are not at all as easy to fathom as it would seem to your conscious minds, and just as often there is benefit to both parties, or in some cases we would have to say all parties. In these cases, continue to do your best to be your best and to open yourself to the changes that are happening. What will invariably happen is that, when your contracts are fulfilled, your built up momentum will propel you forward at a dizzying rate. You are never forgotten, dearest ones.

More problematic, dear hearts, are those who on some level have chosen not to open themselves to change for one reason or another. "Why would I do that?" you say. Perhaps consider asking yourselves, "Why did I do that? Is it more comfortable? Are you afraid of change? There are as many reasons why as there those of you who feel 'stuck'.

And you are not really stuck. At some point you will begin to move if you so desire. But if you really wish to begin moving now, you will need to find a way to confront these things within and see them for what they are. Seeing them is all that is needed. Once you have done that, you will take the next steps almost automatically, asking for help being the first obvious step. Each time one of you dear brothers or sisters takes that first step our hearts rejoice. That is when our work becomes really a joy. But fear not, beloved ones, if you wish to make this journey, make it you will. It is time. The allotted period for this illusion to imprison you has reached its end.

* * * * * * * * * * *

Today we will speak about the impending sea change in your energetic environment.

There has been enough modification to your energy fields now that that almost all of you will know that something of immense importance has happened, and only those who are determined to ignore it will be able to deny that something of significance has occurred. As we are..., I am... informing you of this now, just prior to its occurrence, please be in a state of anticipation and grateful allowance. But please do not expect to awaken to a miraculously changed world.

That will, in fact, be what has happened, but the change will be of an energetic and spiritual nature. We will remind you again that this is what begins everything. When changes of this nature manifest, the outcome in the lower dimensions is, as you put it, "a done deal". This is why we tell you at times that things are happening and you wonder why you cannot see them.

Well, magnificent things are about to occur and many of you **will** see them, but not yet in your physical world. However, as it has been said, for those with the eyes to see, the changes will have been made. The tipping point in the energetic soup in which you live will have been reached, and not by some tiny, unnoticeable shift either. This time, those of you who have become able to sense the energies of which we speak so often will know beyond doubt that something major has happened.

Meantime, there might very well be obvious problems caused by accompanying frequencies, unavoidable, but short-lived. Do not allow yourself to be panicked by those who love to build audience by playing on such emotions. If problems do occur, they will be worked around, as always. The end of the world is not at hand, even if it would sell product and bring more dependence on those who own your major institutions.

Instead, observe, explore, and give thanks for the internal changes you will find activated in yourselves. Some are already seeing glimmers of such things. If you are one of those who do, be prepared to help those around you to make sense of what they are perhaps not quite prepared for. And for the changes you will experience for yourselves, we give our congratulations.

You have worked long and hard, in your waking and sleeping hours, and it is time for you to begin seeing some results and confirmations. There has been a slight calm, a lull if you like, to allow your bodies to prepare. We are about to resume the journey, dear ones.

* * * * * * * * * * *

We will speak today of the continuing success of the lightworkers in opening the understanding and consciousness in your world. We marvel at the ability of so many to avoid seeing what to us is so obvious. Each day now it becomes more difficult to interpret events, and reports of events, in other than a hopeful and positive light.

There are still things occurring which we understand are not so easily understood in this way, but much more is surrounding you which is of a positive nature. Of course the loudest voices are still trumpeting the tune of fear and control. But the strains of peace, progress, freedom, love, and compassion are refusing to be pushed aside any longer. They are there for all to hear if they desire to do so.

Many, many voices are adding themselves to this new chorus every day. Love and light cannot and will not be overridden any longer. As this current continues to pick up steam, it becomes easier and easier for those who have watched and waited to finally make their decisions and join in. Welcome to them.

It is understood that past experiences of pain and suffering have conditioned many to stay out of the fray in self-protection. No blame is attached and no guilt should be felt. Self-preservation is one of the most basic drives of life. You may well find that those ones who have now begun to join in the awakening will throw themselves into the flow with great joy and abandon. They have waited longer and prayed harder for these changes to occur. May they find open arms and open hearts to welcome them.

Look around you often now to find new evidence, however seemingly small, of this rising flood of light. It may be a drop in the ocean, but remember, it is an ocean we speak of. Change your perspective if you are getting discouraged and rise high enough to see the waves. And remember as you give thanks to Creator for creating this, as you give thanks to us for creating this, to give thanks to each other and yourselves, as well. Allow the understanding of All, of One, to enter your hearts.

* * * * * * * * * * *

We wish you to know that the flow of light into this corner of your galaxy, and therefore your planet and yourselves, has once again reached an all-time high. The flow of information is, therefore, also increased. What does this mean for you?

As this light proceeds to flow throughout your energy field and your physical body, you will continue, not begin, but continue, to be enabled, should you choose, to hold more and more of the energy of your true, and shall we say extended, Selves. Your consciousness, memories, perceptions, and all functions thereof will now be able to grow at the extent of your desire.

Yes, it will depend upon your desire, your will, and the state from which you now begin to move forward what that will look like for each of you. But it is not necessary, if it ever was, that you feel 'stuck' any longer. The flow of the energy into and through you is now too great to allow for that unless **you** allow for it. Any earnest effort on your part must now meet with success.

Realize, however, that each of you are 'beginning' from a different place and each of you will have different ideas of what your goals in this process are. Eureka! You now know why there are billions of you here. Create from within yourselves the highest and best and most productive and joyous life you can imagine. Help the person next to you to do the same, whatever that may be. Be in touch, as much as you are able, and as much as you can become able, with your highest understanding of yourselves and your Creator. All else will fall into place as it should, and most likely far better than your imagination was able to foretell. And speaking of your imagination, that most wondrous part of you, turn it loose and see where it may take you.

If it seems to you as if we are a bit more joyous than usual, dear hearts, it is because we see, from our vantage point, that you have once again reached a turning point, and have done so even before we expected you to.

* * * * * * * * * * *

Please accept our congratulations on passing another important marker on your way to higher awareness, greater consciousness. Although you will certainly not feel any different today than you did last week, we can assure you that you are. Each day, hour, and minute that you spend now in the energy field that currently surrounds you sees your entire being becoming more able to contain the higher frequencies that are necessary for your further growth.

There are those around you who do not choose to believe this is occurring. There are those who follow these messages who still think there is nothing happening to themselves, only to others. But, as we have previously stated many times, this energy is having its effect upon everything. We do, however, agree with them in this way. Were they to open themselves to what is possible at this time, welcome the change that is possible for themselves, and feel gratitude for all of it, the potentials for greater and faster manifestation of the life they profess to desire would, as you like to say, knock their socks off.

You can have a little, if that is what you will allow, or you can have a lot. Your wishes will be honored at all times. If you are in conflict about what you wish to allow, you will be given that which you can accept. And, as always, dear friends, you will see what you believe. It is therefore high time for you to clarify, for yourselves, what it is you **do** believe and what you **do** desire.

When we have taught you that you are the co-creators of your lives, it was because it is fact. If you look around you, you will have no problem seeing that in your outside world. Is that not true? Is it not natural then that it be true for you, as well? It is true that you were taught that you did not have such power. And your creation was therefore unconscious. Now you are being told that the power *is* yours. Build the rest of your lives with conscious intention.

We say this not to bring forth any guilt, blame, nor any negative feelings whatsoever. We say it to get you to begin imagining the possibilities that now exist for you. It is not that the manner of creating has changed; it is that your creative energy is being upgraded from regular to high octane. Do not ask us to prove that to you. Look inside and prove it for yourselves.

If you do not know it already, play the game of "if it were true". If it were true, what would you do next? Beginning that process by declaring your intention and gratitude to that which you call your Creator would not be amiss, but start out and see where it will get you. You will astound yourselves. Asking your guides and angels for help is also a good idea, especially if you believe we exist. Yes, we are smiling at that. We live for that possibility, dear friends. It is not necessary for you to be in dire straits before we step in. Just ask.

And one more thing, please begin to consider forgiving yourselves for being who you are. We promise you are each amazing miracles.

* * * * * * * * * *

At the risk of being seen to repeat ourselves endlessly, let us begin by pointing out that once again you are being flooded with vastly more amounts and higher vibrations of light than ever before. You will notice, however, that even though that is so, you are more able to adapt to it than ever before, as well. This is exactly as intended it should be.

The progress being made by you in becoming the new humans that you chose to become is remarkable when you consider the relatively short time in which you have achieved it. Yes, there is still some short way to go, but your evolution is nothing short of amazing.

You will likely have noticed, therefore, that the events of your world are beginning to reflect the new energetic environment in which they are happening. Perhaps they are not completely to your liking yet, at least we hope not, but it would be hard to deny some progress in the right direction. As we have told you over and again, you are the change-makers. Perhaps you do not perceive of yourselves as being on the front lines, so to speak, but we assure you that it is so.

The doing part of the event, as it is a peaceful change we are, and that means you and us, the doing part of the event that we are creating is the doing of energies and intent. No, you very likely will not be written up in any future history books, except those which are spoken of now as the Akashic ones. But in those records, we assure you, you will never be omitted. Your generations, those which are living this time right now, will be told of forever. And may we add this; you are respected and revered even now.

So, dear ones, please do not disrespect yourselves nor sell yourselves short any more. You have a penchant for doing that, you know. You find it easy to read of, and even say that, you are the strongest and the best. But in your hearts, too many of you feel that we must be referring to others. No, my family of earthbound angels, we are referring to you, the one who is reading or hearing this. So, when you enter into your prayers or meditations, endeavor to find and feel the truth of that being, that you, of which we speak in this moment.

We promise you that being, that divine being exists in you and as you. Find her/him, accept these universal energies with gratitude, and watch yourselves grow with ease and grace.

* * * * * * * * * * *

Today we will speak of lighter things. We will speak of the great amount of light which you are absorbing every minute of every hour of your days. We will congratulate you on having brought your world to the very brink of massive but peaceful change.

The Divine has had a huge influence upon this, certainly. But it is you who, as you like to put it, have your boots on the ground that have been making the greatest inroads into the change in the very energy field which creates your reality. Never could this have been done without your intent, your dedication, and your steadfast determination.

You have learned that the most important and far reaching changes are those you make within, and you have never avoided the work that requires. The results of what you have done, and what you continue to do, reach far beyond what you can yet imagine. You have attracted the attention and accolades of everyone in this universe and even beyond.

This has all been told to you before, but on this day, hear it all in one place. Hold this dear to your hearts, dear friends. Use it to reassure yourselves often.

You are now on the very steepest part of your journey. As you well know by now, this is not an easy path to walk. It never has been. But the signs of your impending victory are beginning to appear now.

They will be ignored at first. They will be disguised at times. They will be derided, certainly. But you will see them, and they will be true. Your time of joy is at hand. If you could hear the applause you are receiving even now, it would be deafening.

* * * * * * * * * *

Today we return to happier topics. We will begin by pointing out to you the more positive news that is beginning to enter the reporting in your news media. If you know what has been forecast to occur, you will be able to read between the lines and be encouraged by these things when you see them even though they are not being reported as necessarily positive events. This will continue to accelerate as this year progresses. Efforts are being made to keep you alarmed and off balance, but you have awakened and learned your lessons too well. Your light is spreading, as you knew it would.

We also return to the topic of what is for you incoming energy. It is very strong at present and once again growing stronger. Breathe, my dear friends, breathe. Relax into the changes that are bringing your new world and your new selves to you. Accept them with gratitude and they will cause you much less discomfort.

That lessening of discomfort, if you were experiencing such, will soon transform into a definite feeling of joy and comfort. You will move into a more constructive and less clearing time for your energy fields and your bodies. Your day-to-day lives will begin to reflect this more and more. Your days of personal joy will appear, not with a fanfare, but seemingly as a matter of course.

When you look back, it will seem to bewilder you for a moment perhaps. Or perhaps it will seem like magic. Ah, my dear hearts, you are magical beings, are you not?

This most trying of times, as it seems to many, will have turned out to be your most memorable and joyous. This is your time. Be steady. Be grounded. And be in your hearts as much as you are able. You will find that you have become more and more able to do that.

Ask for our assistance if you need to. Ask for it if you merely want to. Or just feel us around you if you like. We are here. We are always here. Sit with us and enjoy our company. And imagine this. If we were speaking to you, what would we be saying? We are speaking to you, you know. More and more of you are listening. This will become clearer as we move along this road.

* * * * * * * * * *

We congratulate all those who have been, and continue to be, detached from the apparent chaos that surrounds you at this time. As usual, all is not as it appears to be from your perspective.

There is, in fact, a great deal to be joyful about, even in those events which hold so much of your attention if you let them. Of course, we recommend that you not give them that much attention. Still, we recognize the difficulty of that. So let us say that what appears so terrible on the surface is, as we have stated prior to these happenings, only the clearing of the way for much more positive things.

It is now the time for seeing the situations clearly so that beneficial changes can be made later. It is time for the fog to disperse, so to speak. And so it appears that, no matter in which direction you look, there are things which are undesirable to you. That is not any more true than such statements usually are, but it would seem that way, would it not?

May we point out, as has been said, that all of these things are coming up for clearing from your consciousness and your world. In the exposure, they will simultaneously trigger your desires for their replacements. This is how it works.

Release the negativity and place your full attention and intent on the positive outcome. And intend it for all, dear ones. This is the energy which will bring your new world into reality for you. We believe you call it 'greasing the skids'. And trust that we are applying as much or more of the 'grease' than you are. That is our function and our pleasure.

* * * * * * * * * * *

We come today to inform you of the extremely potent flow of energies in which you find yourselves at this time. This was forecast and explained by other sources. It is divinely sent, although you will have noticed that your star and the other heavenly bodies are playing their parts.

That shows the physical component, you see. But understand that the major portion of what we are speaking of is not around you in a form you will be able to measure, at least not yet. But it is something that many of you can sense and even feel.

We assure you that there is no doubt in the minds of any of those who are so gifted. They feel, as well, many changes in their beings and see many changes in their lives. Are they so different?

They are different in the sense that they have looked for and accepted what has been given. All of you are equal in many respects, dear family. But you do not all act is the same ways. This is not to place blame in any wise. It is only to ask you, if you have not done so, to open yourselves fully to these possibilities and to accept them with full knowing that you are deserving and loved.

True, you will begin from the places you are standing. It cannot be any other way. But your rise will be only the more dramatic and joyful if that place you are standing is perhaps no so wonderful, will it not?

And do not be too proud, nor to humble, nor too much in fear or guilt to ask for help. Please, it is the function and joy of your angels to help you. It is the joy of all who are on this side to do whatever we can to be of service. And there is around you and within you, at all times, the unconditional love, the energy, of your Creator. It is available to you in every moment. Call upon it.

Supplication is not what we are talking about, dearest ones. Deserving use of the things of which you are made, that of which you consist, is what we mean. It is what we mean when we say, "Find out who you are." It is the finding of what you are capable of doing that will be the best teacher of that. That is the path upon which you, as a family, have placed your feet. Walk it joyfully as family now.

* * * * * * * * * *

We speak today of the seeming lull which so many feel yourselves experiencing at this time. Many of you feel detached, feel as if you have lost your way, feel as if suddenly the goal is shifting and you cannot perceive it.

We come to tell you that indeed, you are correct in a way. And to tell you there is nothing to worry about. You are receiving a short respite, a rest as it were, after several months of heightened internal changes, many of which you are not even aware... yet. And there have been lately a few weeks of even more stress upon your systems. You needed this rest time and you need also to take advantage of it by enjoying yourselves in whatever you find most rewarding.

There is rapidly approaching another surge, another wave of change, more energy for you to take on and which will continue the changes to yourselves and therefore to your world. As you change, so will your surroundings. As the changes in you become more pronounced, so too will those around you. If you have not quite seen enough yet to make you want to begin your quiet internal celebrations, let us assure you that you soon will. Sorry, we know how very much you love that word 'soon'. What we are observing is that as more and more of you change, the change reaches out to more and more of you. Your word for that is 'exponential'.

And for those who still feel some impatience... we are grinning here because we know none of you are impatient, correct? ... for those who feel some impatience, we say do your best to increase the change in yourselves, as that is overflowing into the rest of your world more and more.

Also, we referenced above a change in goals. What is happening is that many of you are now holding so much more of the energy of your highest and best selves that you are more able to see and feel abilities and possibilities that you could not grasp before. We congratulate you. Possibly those seem a bit unlikely, even impossible, at present. That is alright. Just set them on a mental shelf and do not rule them out just yet. After all, you did not expect to be where you are now just a few short years ago, did you?

You asked for a new world. Why would you expect it to include your old lives? See yourselves there as the highest and best versions of you that you can imagine because, dear ones, that is exactly who will be there.

Now, since some of you do not yet feel us around you, or have not learned to understand the feeling, imagine the kiss on your brow and the hug we send you as we wish you good day.

The Wisdom of Michael

MEDITATION

Meditation will be our topic this morning. Our purpose will be to show you that you can do this as well as anyone else can.

Simplify, please, your perceptions of what meditation is. You have read and heard descriptions of meditational experiences told by others. They tell of things which amaze you, and because none of these things seem to happen to you when you close your eyes, you believe that you cannot meditate and you cease trying in disappointment.

Dear ones, you have lives to live. People, your children and spouses, depend upon you. You have not spent a lifetime in developing this skill, and do not have the time to do so. That is alright. It is understood. If this does not fit, and you are an accomplished meditator, we applaud you. But the overwhelming majority of you will not be cave dwelling hermits nor lifelong meditators. So let us dispel your misgivings and give you a chance to use this magnificent tool to move yourselves forward from wherever you are.

And that phrase is key, my friends, wherever you are. It is impossible to begin a journey from anywhere else than wherever you are. So here is a new goal we propose you adopt. "I will meditate each day." It is very simple. It is where to start.

You will learn more, just as you have in every other area of your life. You may indeed find yourself at some time having those marvelous visions and experiences. That this may happen is not important. What is important is for you to find, in your hearts, peace and freedom to know yourselves for who you truly are. And of those two things, we emphasize peace. It is very hard to achieve that in your world. And when you are able to feel that, you do, in fact, share it with all others, whether you know it or whether you do not.

Now, since you are reading or listening to this message on an electronic device of some sort, we tell you that it is perfectly fine for you to use the thousands and thousands of meditational sound tracks and videos to guide and help you in this process. Your mission, should you choose to accept it, is to spend time each day with you and only you. We add a little humor to lighten this up. It should be light. We are offering you a release and a relief, not a new chore. You should feel, "Ah, now I can meditate for a bit," not "Now I have to meditate."

Peace and self-discovery--make those the only considerations--and you will have done wonders for yourselves. Make this first step and we promise you that in very short order you will miss it on the days when you need to skip it. And, by the way, do not beat yourselves up over that either.

* * * * * * * * * *

Grounding. Grounding and centering. A new month is now upon you, my dear friends, in which we cannot stress enough the importance of these practices. Walk in nature, if that is available to you. Meditate and ground your energies with gratitude to your dear mother, Earth. However you have learned to do these things, do them now.

We have told you that, when things began to move, they would accelerate rapidly. Well, they have started, and they are about to accelerate. We do not want to have you left with your heads spinning. We also do not want, and this is most important, anyone to be put into fear or anger by what will begin to happen. This is one of the main purposes of messages of this sort.

We have been foretelling of these events for several years now. We have heard you saying, "Bring it on! We are ready!" Well, it is not exactly us bringing it on. You are the co-creators here. But you have brought it on, just as we have told you. Do not now say, "Oh, no! What shall I do?" Omelet making time is here and you are breaking eggs.

We are teasing you. Allow us a bit of humor. As the Japanese would say, "Pull up your fundoshi (diaper) and get on with it." Or in America, "Put on your big girl panties." OK. Serious now. Things are going to heat up in your near future. You will see some things which are meant to raise fear and anger in you. That is their purpose. Do not let that happen.

You have made wondrous strides. Maintain your focus and do not let any efforts to throw you off meet with success. If you feel the need for support, please ask us. That is why we are here. Support each other, as well.

Also, we see that some are beginning to experience a few rather disconcerting things with their sight, hearing, etc. If you are, you are not going crazy. You are evolving. If you are not, you are not being left behind. You will all advance in the best way for yourselves. You cannot begin from anywhere other than where you are. And what you do not need, you will not experience. It is not being done to you. It is being done for you, and by you. Trust the process. Better yet, trust your selves. You will, one day soon, realize quite a bit more of who those selves really are.

WE ARE ONE

We think it is time to point out to you the remarkable increase in your understanding of the information in your possession. Things which you have had in your intellect for many years are beginning to make sense. Things which seemed to be at best mythical are beginning to fit into your world of possibilities. Your understanding, and we say 'your' as in humanity's, is beginning to broaden immensely. Information previously hidden is beginning to come into the consciousness of the populations.

From your individual perspective, this may appear as a trickle or a surge. From the larger view, this is nothing less than a tsunami. It took over one hundred years for the great discoveries of the early twentieth century to mold the world you now live in. That was a massive change. There are people alive today whose grandparents saw the first motion picture, airplane, automobile, television, and telephones. They never lived to see a personal computer, much less the Internet. Some of them saw the first moon landing. All of this happened in one hundred years.

We tell you now that the amount of change you will see now and in the next handful of years will far surpass that. It is beginning where it must begin, in you. You created the world you are living in and you will create the next one as well. So mark well the changes that are taking place within yourselves. That is where you will begin to see the kind of world you will be living in.

If nothing had changed, you would have seen this world destroy itself. Well, you would have destroyed her. You will now be able to see how much you have changed by first noticing that you have not done that, and then by watching yourselves turn this back into the unbelievably beautiful garden that she was created to be. And when you begin to see that happen, remember this, it will be a reflection of who you are.

Look around you now and begin the process by imagining that you see nothing that does not contain a part of the consciousness of the Creator, that there is nothing you see which is not deserving of love, respect, and appreciation. And, dear ones, it can respond to that as well as you, yourselves, do. You may have to begin by imagining that, but you will discover soon enough that it is in fact the truth. Play with that thought in your meditations and in your lives and see where it takes you.

Here is a hint. We are one. We are the One. We tell you nothing at all new. You will only find that head slapping eureka moment. And you will have those moments very often now. And that is all because of the 'nothing' that happened at the end of your last year. Welcome to your new world, dearest friends. As your songwriter said, "The times, they are a-changin'."

* * * * * * * * * * *

Synchronicities, feathers, coins, and signs of all kinds abound at this time. We are doing everything we can to get your attention. We are here and we are working with you in every way we are able. If you are open to the possibility, ask and you will receive all the signs you need that we are indeed with you.

There is much, much more to reality than you know or even imagine. You have spent over a hundred years searching for the 'missing link'. Did they but know it; it is at last beginning to be acknowledged by your scientists. Consciousness is that link. Consciousness is everywhere. Energy is everything. At its core, matter is no more solid than thought is. All is love.

How much is understood now that was totally foreign to the thinking of mankind so recently. Of course, in many places only the very few think of these things at all. But that is changing, as well. In your quiet inner moments, dwell on these things, dearest ones. More than things to pass through your mind, what do they mean?

Could it be that nothing separates you from any other thing? Could it be that nothing really separates you from me? Could you possibly know what I want you to know before you read these pages? Is there a level at which we are indeed all One?

What would that mean in the context of daily life? All are equal? Indeed, dear ones. All are worthy? All are loved? All are precious? No one and nothing is less than? Most of all you, in your being, are precious, worthy, and loved beyond measure.

You are exactly as you need to be at this moment. It may take some time for you to allow this become your true belief and feeling, but we assure you that it must be and will be your truth at some point. Claim it now; it has never been untrue, even when you have felt so.

All of the pain, all of the suffering, exist because you have allowed the belief of your being less than, of being undeserving, of being unloved and unworthy to live in your hearts. It is time now for you to awaken from that nightmare.

Ask! Allow! Listen! Learn to love yourself as the son or daughter of the One. There are those of you who will feel these words deeply. We tell you that from the moment you realize this, we will walk with you and hold your hand as you find your way out of the dream. Your Creator has no interest whatsoever in seeing you suffer and never has had. You are deeply loved.

* * * * * * * * * *

We bring to your attention today two familiar concepts that you may find much easier to understand and feel the truth of now than ever before. The first is that you are each and all part of one consciousness, one conscious field.

The second, and the one which we would urge you now to actually feel the truth of, is that you are far larger than the physical body which you have chosen to inhabit. As a matter of fact, your body is in the field which is you, and not the other way around.

This concept is likely not new to most of you, but with the energizing of your fields, which is ongoing at his time, it is quite likely that, if you close your eyes and place your attention on this possibility, you will be easily able to discern, by your feeling of your own energy, the truth of it. What you are able to feel at this time will, for most of you, still be only a slight beginning, as we tell you that your energy field stretches into the infinite oneness, but it will be a beginning.

Spend time with this. Allow your imagination to play with this. See where it leads you. See how this second idea leads you right back into the first, that you are each a part of the one consciousness. And, now that you are there, allow as much of the full meaning of that to enter your minds as you are able to handle at this time. There will be much more, certainly, but again, it is a start.

In this space you are, you see, not separate from he, not separate from she, and not separate from any of us. Might we suggest that, from this space, you allow unconditional love to permeate the entire being that you are, which we are. Drink this into your soul, into your every cell. Again, spend time with this. Love that which you are. There will be eternities for you to love that which you wish to become. Today love that which you are in gratitude and appreciation. That which you call Creator does. Can you do less?

WORTHINESS

You have reached the end of a short period of rest, which we gather from our channel, you really were not all that comfortable with.

It is time now for you to assess the tools available to you and to determine what your contributions will be. Are you truly ready to begin? If it all breaks loose tomorrow, can you say that you truly are ready? Because, my dear friends, tomorrow is here.

We have stated many times through our trusted channels that this season would be the time in which things would be ready to begin, and they are. We have said that we awaited a certain point to be reached and a signal to be given. There is now no further reason to wait.

But there is one teensy consideration to take into account. What will you do? It need not be something as grandiose as, "I will change the world!" But you should know by now what you love to do and how it might contribute to a better place for all. There are, after all, several billions of you to make such contributions. And there are right now, many millions of you ready to start.

So look deeply into your hearts and simply declare "This is the start!" It takes no more than that, my friends. This is the start. Perhaps add frequently, "Is this helping?" A good question to begin with, don't you think? And then, dearest ones, if it is not, make a change.

And do a thing for yourselves, please. Start giving yourselves credit for being worthy and deserving when we tell you that you are. Think. The universe had many trillions of volunteers to come and do this job. You are here. Why is that, do you suppose? Stop wasting your valuable energies beating yourselves up and apply them to the task at hand. Not all of you do that, by any means, but far too many do. Not only is the past long over, not only are you the only one concerned with it, but you are needed now to do much greater things.

Look around, not outside, but in your hearts, and realize that the only judge in sight is yourself. Even assuming that there was once something that you needed to judge yourself for, and there was nothing there dear one but illusion, forgive it. Drop it. Let it go. Your Creator has long since forgiven you. Won't you do the same?

Now! Look out at the future and see how much brighter it appears. You see, all of that past taught you many, many things. You are expert in many of them. You are. Don't worry. They will surface when needed. Just begin. Make today better. Imagine that happening by a power of millions. Do it again tomorrow. Here we go, dearest angels. Here we go.

* * * * * * * * * * *

We have noticed, and would speak for a moment about, a very gratifying development. More and more in these recent days, ideas which were introduced by this channel and others are being accepted and spoken of by others. This, of course, is the whole purpose of our communications, and it both makes those of us doing the communicating happy, and bodes very well for the increasing progress toward your goals.

Ideas, like precious seeds, must be planted, nurtured, and cared for carefully until they become strong enough to thrive, and that has happened, though you may not notice in your day-to-day rushing about. This is true over your entire globe, also, and not just in the few places which read and speak your particular language, whatever that may be.

And since we have mentioned it, your rushing about is becoming a bit less hectic, as well. All this meditating and walking in nature is having a wonderful effect upon you, is it not? You see, when you are doing that, you are, as you say, unplugged. And not only are you benefitting from the higher and more peaceful energies, but you have withdrawn your own energies from the support of the old. You are plugging in to the building of the new.

Every single time one of you does this, a cause is made and an effect is created. Every time you do this you become just that much more sensitive and able to feel the change in yourselves and your surroundings.

Every thought of peace, of abundance, of joy, of freedom, of love, is a pebble laid upon the growing mountain of intent. Multiply this in your imagination by the millions of you who are now awakening and you will see the new world you desire rising before your eyes. Truly it is an amazing sight to behold. You are an amazing sight to behold. And those of you who have already begun to contact your guides and teachers are being apprised of that fact if you will allow such into your consciousness.

We wish you to discover your own worth, your own worthiness, your deservedness, and make it your own, own it as you say. You have been taught otherwise long enough. You have believed otherwise long enough. Seek that wondrous you within now. It is no longer so deeply buried.

* * * * * * * * * *

Today we bring your attention once again the topics of self-worth and deservedness. There is no possibility that too much stress can be put upon, nor too much attention paid to these subjects. They indeed are things which almost all of you do not feel and cannot believe. Why is that?

It is because you have indeed judged yourselves when even your divine Creator has not, nor will He ever judge you. And you have many times asked for forgiveness for that which you have judged yourselves guilty of, yet mostly refused to accept forgiveness of yourselves, from yourselves.

You have heard it told you over and over that you are divine beings, co-creators with the All. You nod your heads sagely. Yet you cannot find the real belief of that in your hearts.

But now, dear angels on Earth, around the edges of the veil you have hidden behind all these millennia, comes a growing light. Now comes the possibility, the maybe. Skills, feelings, thoughts, and memories that have been unfamiliar to you for countless lifetimes are peeking through. You feel the urge often to turn away as you always have done. Yet more and more you find yourselves beginning to accept the possibility of the truth. Am I? Could I be? Will I be?

We tell you once again, hoping that this time you will accept, with no reservations, the message that has ever been given. More than one messenger has given a life to bring this to you. Hear it now. You, dear one that is reading this, are a divine face of the ONE. You hold within your heart, no matter who you are, where you are, or what you have or have not done, a portion of the perfect love and life of the Creator of ALL.

By extension of that thought, you are a part of the Creator, as is every other life in the universe. There is nothing which you lack. There is nothing of which you can dream which is not possible. If there is anything to which you might need to exert yourselves, it is in the acceptance, allowance, and realization of this truth. Turn your attention to the finding of this within you.

You, your neighbor, your world, and your universe are waiting with bated breath for you to make this realization now. We are waiting. And we and uncounted others are sending love and light as never before in the grandest effort you can imagine in support of your efforts. We see your success as an accomplished fact. You are still waiting. Well, it is flooding into you now. Allow it and celebrate it. If your circumstances seem to deny it, turn its flood of energies upon those circumstances. It is real. The circumstances are not.

Love and light are real. They will go where you send them. That, dearest ones, is who and what you are in the most basic of terms. Our celebrations of you have begun, but we still stand ever in support and comfort of you whenever you ask.

MISCELLANEOUS

Welcome to your new age. Is there not a feeling of newness around you? Some are having difficulty orienting themselves in such a different internal environment. You will have yourselves anchored firmly soon.

There is a feeling of the world holding its breath to see what will happen. Also, it seems that the whirlwind you lived in for so long had begun to subside. There is a feeling of calmness, of quiet. It is time allowed you for an assessment of who you are, of what you want to do, for a flexing of your internal muscles. Time to learn how to walk in your newness, dear ones.

For many, it is time to realize there is a newness. Some dear ones will be surprised at new feelings, at what comes out of their mouths. Some final adjustments are still being made. That is causing quite a few of you to sleep far more than you were used to. It will pass quickly.

You may begin now to remember more and more of what passes in your dream states. Formerly, you have been unaware of how you passed a great deal of your lives. That is not so necessary anymore. You have hidden a great deal from yourselves that will gradually begin to surface now. Also, the abilities of many to expand their awareness of what is around them will become more and more obvious. There is a wonderful newness and beauty to your world. We invite you to open to it.

Listen to your inner promptings and let the old restrictions that you accepted years ago to drop away. Be a child again. We are loving what we see as you begin to understand and get your bearings. Gather yourselves and assess your dreams anew. Begin to look at them as new possibilities.

* * * * * * * * * * *

It is our joyous opportunity today to report to you your remarkable progress. You have taken stock of the true situation in which you have found yourselves and, as always, have reached down into the deepest reserves of your being and discovered the amazing strength which resides there. You have stood up and are ready to stride out once again upon the paths you have chosen.

True, some have still not been able to do this, but your examples will show them that things are far better than they appear. There was a very steep and dangerous stretch of the journey that needed to be covered in the last few years, and you all have succeeded very, very well. Now many are discovering, as they assess where they are, that they have not only grown immeasurably, but have gained some things they never thought they would.

This is why some tell you to always remember to add "or something better" to the end of your prayers. There is usually something better when the goal is limited to what you can imagine. And many have begun to leave the "how" part out of their prayers. This is wonderful, also. Believe us, any "how" that you can dream up is nothing but restrictive compared to all the possibilities at the universe's disposal. Your conscious mind is finally learning to tend to the business for which it was designed.

It helps a great deal when you discuss with each other the successes you have and what you learn from them. Something which may seem small or unimportant to you could well be the next big thing another needs to think about. Your progress does indeed change the whole, but your sharing directly might save another quite a bit of effort.

As always we offer our support in all things. Call on us and on your personal guides much more than you do. It is, after all, what we are here for.

* * * * * * * * * * *

It is time now for humanity to begin the creation of your new world. You have weathered the ups and downs of the initial period of heavy upgrades to your energetic and bodily systems and are ready now to step ahead into the real work that you came here to do.

Some of you have already chosen projects and ideas to work on. That is a wonderful thing. Let us in no way slow you down from such things. The main work for most of you at this time, however, is to continue clearing out any and all of the old clutter from your minds and lives. Then ask yourselves what you truly wish to accomplish from this point forward.

Take no notice of your age, your 'qualifications', or anything else other than your true heart's desire. You may save nations, dear hearts, or you may have an effect upon a family, even an individual, during your time here. But what the effect of that may be upon the future of this world, you cannot begin to know. How many kindnesses, words of wisdom, or gestures of compassion have, completely unknown to the ones who contributed them, turned people, nations, and history around in the past? Stories of these things have amazed you over and over again.

The point of the stories is that you might be the one to create that next miracle. But in order to do that, you must be ready. How are you to be ready, do you imagine? Just continue to be and become the very best you that it is possible for you to become. No one can ask more of you than that. None expect more of you than that. It is, after all, the reason you are here. Do you know what that contribution may be? We are sure you do not.

You love affirmations, we observe. Try this one if you will. "I am where I need to be, when I need to be there, to do what I need to do when I need to do it." Let us, and your life, take care of the rest.

There is more we need to discuss soon, but this is enough for today. Stay grounded and grateful for all that is being showered upon you now. Yes, it continues to rise in intensity, but as we have told you, you are becoming more and more able to assimilate it.

* * * * * * * * * * *

Today let us consider your current situation and help you to feel a bit better about it.

Remember that your current situation is the moment or moments prior to your next situation. It is the time in which causes have been made, and are being made, which will yield later results. It is also the time in which your thoughts, decisions, and intentions are the real power of which you have been so often apprised, and which you find so hard to understand.

This moment, **this moment**, is one in which you could actually be celebrating what you have done if you could see what it truly contains. That is because, unless you change your minds, the work to produce the next moment has been done.

And why can we see that and you cannot? Well, you see, you have invented a really wonderful way keep yourselves from making instant and possibly painful mistakes by not being able to see the results of your actions and intentions, thus giving yourselves a chance to reconsider and learn. It was a good and useful idea which you are about to find you have outgrown.

You created a focus so minute that you could see only a very limited field of what you formerly could perceive. You call it time. You see cause, pause, and then effect. For those who do not so limit themselves, the effect is inherent in the cause. It is already.

But very soon, when you have sufficiently allowed your consciousness to expand, you will begin to see the inherent effects of the causes and not need this linear time illusion any longer. Except that you had decided to create this separation game, you never did need it to begin with, but much has been learned and nothing should be regretted. Others are still lost in the game and you are to have the opportunity to use the wisdom you have gained to help them as you have been helped.

Some are now feeling a very sharp rise in the energies you are entering. They are correct. Smile, breathe, and enjoy the ride. In keeping with our penchant for injecting a bit of humor into these messages, please keep your arms and legs within the earth vehicle until we have arrived at our destination.

* * * * * * * * * * *

We wish to spend some time today discussing your money and economies. It is rather unique to your world to do things in the manner you have chosen. On other worlds, everyone contributes to the society, of course. Without that, there really would not be a society, would there? However, you have chosen to make the basic necessities of life, the food, shelter, clothing, and education needed to live in your societies, those things which are essential to each and every individual, into salable goods. There really is no compassion there, is there?

Then you have allowed the control of the supply of that one item, money, to be placed, or rather taken, by truly a handful of individuals. You have literally given it away, rather than maintain it, once you had wrested it free from the grasp of a king. And then the system they invented to take control spread like a virus.

You see the problem lay in your allowing yourselves to believe them when they told you that they knew what was good for you. You began by saying, "Go and run our country as we wish it to be run", and allowed it to become, "Go and run our country so we won't have to."

Now the question is whether or not you have realized your mistake in time. What do you think? Have you done so? We are speaking of one country, but the same situation has, as we have said, spread like the virus that it is. Have you awoken in time? It does not appear to be so, does it? But take heart, dearest angels. As you are fond of saying, things are never as they seem.

The problem for you now, in that regard, is that what you see is, in most cases, only what the controlling interests want you to see. That is because they have conveniently arranged to own the means of distributing information. They really are brilliant in some ways, you know. However, in their infatuation with themselves, they have made one or two little errors. They overreached, and they believed they could be more powerful than the life force itself. One cannot overpower what one is actually a part of. Doesn't that make sense? And each created being is a part of the whole, the One.

So things are destined to turn out a bit differently than they planned. This situation has been allowed to continue to the point that will cause the corrections necessary to give you a bit of a bumpy ride though. We wish that were not so, but it is. This is what results in your wishing for an outside force to come in and save you from yourselves. But the universe is not set up that way, my dear friends.

In your case, however, it has been decided that your initiation of corrections, your intent and your involvement are enough to invite help from others. Many of the others are here now, in spirit, in other dimensions, in short, in ways which make them not quite visible to you. That is also information which has been carefully kept from you.

Ideas such as these have been laughed at and scoffed at until you dared not express them. Well, there are a lot of things that have been scoffed at up until now which are about to take center stage in this little game. And we predict with certainty that you will enjoy the result.

Now, up until today, statements like that have always caused an outcry of 'whens' and 'bring-it-ons'. And we have repeatedly replied that you must take responsibility for the initiation of events. And then there was a bit of timing involved, as well. We believe you can begin now to sense the pot beginning to boil.

If you are not one of those who have taken the initiatives involved, do not be dismayed. Your own progress has been a part of the change in consciousness needed as well. Do not let up now, my friends. In fact, it is time to redouble and reaffirm. Determine now to keep your head when all about you are losing theirs. Things will get a bit squirmy in a bit. Do not lose hope. Trust yourselves to come out the other side. And at that time, we promise you; you will have made a system which allows for the compassionate care of every individual on your world, just as you have dreamed. Dreams, you see, are not the silly things you have been told they are. Not much is as you have been told it is.

* * * * * * * * * * *

Our focus today will be on focus. For a very many reasons this is important for you at this time. It is a critical tool in your toolbox, both for achieving your objectives of raising your energy and frequency, and for your protection, allowing that to happen in the best and easiest way.

We ask you to focus, to a much higher degree, upon your path and upon your intent to always, in every

117

moment, be feeling good. We ask you to focus on finding more and more ways to feel good about yourselves. We ask you to focus more and more on feeling unconditional love for all around you.

Why, other than the obvious reason that it is what you need to be doing to create a better life for you and others, do we ask this now? We said it concerned your protection. We wish you to focus so exclusively on these things that you do not have time to give any attention to the negative things which are occurring outside the sphere of your own particular world at this time.

Much effort is being put into distracting you. We speak to all who call themselves workers for the light— all who are giving the most effort they can to manifesting a new world that is in the highest and best interests of all. It is critical to those who wish to maintain the status quo that your efforts, your energies be distracted from that task. You see—you are much too successful. That is the reason for their desperate efforts to place you into a state of fear. Be in a state of love, dearest friends, and you will not be the ones in a state of fear.

And be not in a state of love in order to place others into a state of fear but to show them the state of love into which they can place themselves at any moment they decide to change. That is the true way.

If you have found something for you to do, then devote all your attention and might into doing. If you are still waiting to discover a thing to do, then be, dear hearts. Be that being of unconditional love which you truly are and all else will be done as it needs to be.

This is what more and more of you are learning each and every day now. Awaken. Awaken to the truth of who and what you are. This, I, Michael, and we, your protectors, angels, and counselors will aid you with in every step of your way. You have only to ask.

* * * * * * * * * * *

Today we wish to discuss the phenomenon of growing and connecting groups of lightworkers and wayshowers. In times past, and even until very recently, it has been very common for you to have found yourselves isolated in places where you were a true outpost for the light, holding and anchoring the new energy in spite of all odds, even in the face of ridicule. You felt completely alone. Let us tell you now that your efforts have produced far more effect than you yet realize.

The trickle of building energy, of increasing numbers of you, through awakenings and births, has reached the point where such isolation is no longer necessary, and in fact, there are very likely now better uses for the energies you carry. Even the most aware of you do not understand yet the full impact of your energy upon your environment, but we tell you it can make, and has made all the difference.

We wish for you now to begin giving yourselves credit where credit is due. We do not mean for you to go about "blowing your horn", as you put it. Rather we mean for you to stand erect and realize that, in large part, the new world that is coming into being is due to your intent and perseverance, which returns us to the ongoing theme of 'love yourselves'.

You will find, within the near future, that you are no longer alone. You may find yourselves in new places. Certainly, you will be among those much more receptive to your understandings and those of like hearts and minds. Remember to bring to them your love and joy. It is quite possible they have felt as alone as you have.

In due time, you will begin to find the reasons for your new groups to emerge upon the societal horizon. You are the seeds of growing trees, even forests. Stand proud. Offer love. The rest will take care of itself.

Remember that we are always closer than your next thought. We support your every moment. We are there when you need us. And we are not and cannot be too busy to hear you.

* * * * * * * * * * *

We wish you to know that that which you have worked for so long, and with such dedication, has now commenced. You have been informed of this from other sources, as well, and we confirm for you that this information is correct.

You know that the messages you have followed, those which you have discerned to be most reliable and loving, have shown a tendency to converge in their content in recent months. That, dear ones, dearest and most loyal hearts, is because the basic message *is* the same, as it always has been. The message now is short and oh so sweet. The freedom, abundance, prosperity, and total transformation of your world, which you have prayed for these last thousands of years, and which has been incomprehensibly denied you, is now to be yours.

There is now, due to your intent, perseverance, and growth to occur a season of change such as you have never dreamed of. We do not promise it will be easy. In fact, it promises to be quite unsettling for many. However, for those ones, you will be the anchor and the calming influence you have the capability to be, and all will be well.

Let peace be the intent and love be the way, and all will be well. We think no more need be said at this time. We wish not to dilute this message. However, we will be speaking with you again and often, as we have been.

Let the celebration in your hearts begin. Find your joy and hold it close. Maintain your resolve. Wrap yourselves in our loving embrace. We are here in your hearts, as we have always been. You have always asked for evidence in your world of the truth of this. Such evidence you shall have.

* * * * * * * * * * *

It is time for us to discuss the movements that are occurring in your societies. Others have done so. Even other channelings have done so. But we have only touched upon the topic here. This may be a short message, but we trust you will give it thought and consideration.

You see around you now reports of much upheaval. You are told of riots, of massive protests, of government crackdowns. You are apprised almost daily of plans and technologies that are meant to control you even more than you are at present controlled. You are bombarded endlessly with stories of mayhem of all sorts, most of which, may we point out, has occurred many thousands of miles away from you. If you are following these things, it is very easy for you to lose yourselves in feelings of doubt, fear, and depression.

Most of those following these messages, not all, but most, have learned to balance what they take into their consciousness and remain hopeful and centered in themselves. Even so, we have a point we wish to make regarding all of this.

You are, at present, beginning to reconstruct your world into the type of place that the very biggest majority of you have longed and prayed for across the last several thousand years. You have asked for it, and it is time for it to happen. Your world is now a construction site, my friends. But we cannot build a safety fence around it to keep you from experiencing the turmoil. We cannot issue hardhats. You are living in the middle of the work area. What we can do is help to remember the truth about what is going on if you will only give some little credence to our words.

Everything that you now see, no matter how it appears on its surface, is being used to bring about the changes you desire and, in fact, are creating for yourselves. So if you must look at the more disturbing things, and we certainly think you should not bury your heads in the sand as you say, then we ask you to look for the possible ways in which they may contribute to the desirable outcome. Mostly, try to remain aware at these times of the changes in the world consciousness which they are bringing about. They have certainly made a great impact on your own, have they not?

In the meantime, continue to work on your own growth and to offer whatever love and comfort you can to others. Such love, we offer, IS the new world you long for.

* * * * * * * * * * *

Today we wish to speak of the reticence of those in positions of power to relinquish their positions even when confronted by the will of the masses of people whom they think they govern.

You are being made aware of these protests by your social networks and alternative news sources even though there is still precious little about them in your newspapers or on your television networks. For yourselves, we urge you to combine all of the reports you do see into as complete a picture as you can. You will become aware that this is a huge movement indeed, and this has not escaped the attention of those who would control you from behind closed doors.

Our message today is twofold. First we would point out to the men behind the curtain that this is a force that is becoming so large that they cannot possibly control it. Stemming the tide in one location will not stop the tide itself.

Secondly, for those of you who support and pray for the success of what is occurring, we would point out the following. Even though you are vastly in the majority, you can bring down upon yourselves vast resources that you have given to your governments. This is not at all desirable. You can and will achieve your aims peacefully if you so choose. Your peaceful actions will surely show each breach of peaceful behavior by those who stand in your way in the worst possible light. Something they also are aware of.

That is the reason they sometimes insert agents into your own ranks to stir up violence. Be aware of these tactics and expose them whenever you see them. For those not directly involved, and we wish that could be every one of you, please support peaceful and loving success with each beat of your hearts. We assure you that even if that were all that happened, it would be enough to insure the outcome. Nevertheless, send unconditional love to all involved.

We stress 'unconditional' and 'all involved'. There is no one involved on either side of these situations that is not a divine child of the universe, regardless of his or her beliefs or actions. Therefore, let your prayers be for all. Perhaps just let your prayers be for the wondrous new world you and they are building.

Call upon the support of any or all of us, and it shall certainly be yours. We hold love and admiration in our hearts for every dear soul who has placed herself or himself on your Earth at this time. You are the New Earth. Be safe, well, and at peace.

* * * * * * * * * *

The time has now come for you to accept your own divine nature. It will now become increasingly important, as well as easier, for you to do this. Do not, however, confuse this with an increase in the less desirable traits of your ego natures. This is not to be reasoned with your intellects, but felt in your hearts. And when felt there, to be accepted by you, to be acknowledged.

It is no longer a time when playing small, when believing the incorrect concepts about your natures is in your best interests. Of course it never was, but your world now needs your abilities and your better selves as much as you do. Telling you this will quite likely awaken any remaining dread, fear, and doubt that still linger in your hearts. Look at them squarely, thank them for their service in keeping you from the fray in prior times, and send them home to be reborn as courage, confidence and belief in yourselves.

Do not rest until you have found the feeling of self-worth that will arise when you understand at last who you truly are. You really did ask to come here. You truly did desire to witness and participate in this unfolding. You truly are the very best choices for this time. You are.

Feel these words in your heart and cherish them. Feel, as well, the boundless love that we send you as you read this. Build in your hearts a special place to keep this feeling. Knowing that you will need to feel it many times, store it there for your future. We will keep it replenished with love and power, with the eternal support which is ours to give.

We do not urge you to do anything other than what your own personal heart feels that you need to do. Let that, which is guided by your own history and understanding, be your guide. You are each as unique as the grains of sand. That is as it should be, and it is what is needed. Just be yourselves, but begin now to be the very best selves that you can imagine. And know, as we do, that you are never, never alone in the process.

It is possible to be humble and proud at the same time. Be proud of who you are and humble in your manner. Your time is now.

* * * * * * * * * *

We would love to speak about another topic this day, but events upon your world make it almost mandatory that we address what is uppermost in everyone's mind.

It has been placed there by the unceasing attention of those who are trying, with every means possible to keep you tuned in to their broadcasts of fear and control. You have begun to see through the web of illusion they have spun for so long. The mothers of those sent to an ill fate have long seen this for what it is, but of course it has been possible for long times past to relegate their opinions and concerns to the back of your mass consciousness. Still today, in many places, the saying, "It's a man's world" rings too true.

Your hearts and your minds have been manipulated very effectively for thousands of years. Even your teachings that speak of love and peace have been twisted into the service of control and profit. Love has been twisted into hate. Peace has become something to fight for.

We see, however, that the effects of the movement of your planet into the higher energies of the universe, what you are seeing as your new age, has resulted already in the awakening of masses of people to the truth and the strengthening of their resolve to cease such obviously hurtful behavior, hurtful to yourselves and disastrous to your world. We know that a point will be reached which will see this behavior end.

We know that you will regain control of your own lives. This is the will of the Divine and it is a given.

There is still a variable involved, however. And that variable is this. When will you make that happen, dear ones? When will you realize that you are the true owners of your own lives? Many have done so already. Examples have been shown.

We see that the degree of comfort is being surpassed by the degree of discomfort. Are you hoping for that to cease without any action on your part? Are you waiting for a proverbial 'them' to do something?

We suppose we have said enough this day. Please consider deeply what we have discussed. And do not mistake anything we have said as criticism, please. We know who you were, who you are, and who you are becoming. How then could we not love you without measure?

* * * * * * * * * * *

We return now to discuss what is happening for many of you at this time.

Your purposes, your abilities, and your perceptions of opportunity are coalescing into something which seems more possible to you than before. What was once not even thought of is coming into focus for you.

Many of you feel surprise as this happens for you. Do not be surprised. Before the changes that have been given you, many of these things would not have been possible. But now, you are taking up the tools which your past experience and current intent have given you. All of the talent you have so arduously earned is returning. The vision may still be a bit fuzzy for a while yet, but it will clear. Circumstances that you came into your lives to take care of, opportunities you foresaw, will appear around you. You will be prepared.

Some of these may seem huge and daunting, some may simply seem mundane, but every one of them, each of your lives, is now and will be necessary to make up the whole. This has ever been true and it is still true today. So step forth, dear friends, knowing that each smile, kind word, and loving thought is building, more rapidly than ever, the world you envision. And if you now begin to feel the pull to begin something new, do so with all your heart.

We will support you every step of the way. Only ask. Continue to go within and listen peacefully to what your heart tells you is your way, your path, your joy. It is your time.

It has been a difficult climb for many of you to this point. The path will begin to level out now.

* * * * * * * * * *

Today we will speak on a wonderful subject, progress, and more specifically, your progress.

We intend merely to draw your attention to something which you pay scant attention to. And so, we will, as we say, call your attention to your own individual states of being, of your consciousness now. It is more than a little likely that those of you who read these and other such messages can barely recollect what you were like just twelve of your months ago.

We remind you that you were in a fervor over what would occur on the 21st day of that month. Then, you were mostly disappointed that 'nothing' happened due to your inflated expectations of what that date might bring. Even the explanations that were made during the next few weeks seemed to you to be only excuses of our channels. The higher densities from which these messages come have no need of excuses, but we do see that some wisdom was gained at that time. That is not the subject we intend to discuss now, however.

During these past months, you have been bombarded over and again with steadily increasing amounts of energetic frequencies which you barely are beginning to understand. In one sense, these run the entire gamut of the higher energies that your world is moving through. In another sense they can be summed up with the term Unconditional Love.

You have many other phrases to name this, zero point, source field, and morphogenetic field being among them. But this is what has been and will continue to be available to all who wish to advance, to evolve, or, as your favorite term calls it, to ascend. This is what has produced changes in you which you can hardly define, changes which you did not see happening.

You might wish to look back now and assess the difference in your overall feeling of your being. We see, from our perspective, that your entire planet has a higher energy signature than it has had for a very long time, the highest in what you would call your recorded history. Imagine this higher energy, this unconditional love radiating out from you into the collective consciousness of your world, and see it also being absorbed from without as we immerse you in it, as well.

We spoke some months ago of snowball effects, of avalanches, and of waterfalls. We told you that would best describe the rate of change which you would see in your near future. Then we told you that it had begun and that it would continue to increase. Most of you now are able, through your own personal experience, to see this now. You have changed and are still changing, and still we say, "You haven't seen anything yet."

So we invite you to include that in your celebration of this always joy filled holiday season. Celebrate yourselves. We join you in that and look forward to sharing these last incredible few days of your year with you.

COUNCILS

Our message today begins with our congratulations to the channel on his safe and successful move to his new home. We know that he is aware of all the help we were able to provide in that endeavor, and we are gratified that he accepted that help with open heart and mind. Much will be accomplished now.

Our main topic for this message will be, in fact, the help that we can provide now when one discovers and moves onto the path toward fulfilling his or her life contracts. We wish that a new word could be used for that, as it implies things in your current usage that do not apply; however, the word will do for now.

These contracts do not have penalty clauses. There is only the promise of fulfillment when they are completed. And let us state now that they are subject to being changed or "upgraded" as your lives progress and your external and internal situations change. The Councils, as they have been called, in which these contracts are agreed upon are always, always in session, and you visit them regularly, if you but knew it.

Very soon, as measured in our consciousness, you will become much more aware of these things, and your feelings of having things thrust upon you by fate will dissipate accordingly. Nothing, of course, is, or has ever been, thrust upon you. You are and have always been a free and divine entity. Your circumstances have, at all times, been in agreement with your choices, but your choices and the memories of your reasoning have been hidden from yourselves, by yourselves, in order to learn lessons that you felt you needed. You will be ecstatic when you discover what you have accomplished by this, and you have not much longer to wait before the 'awakening', as you call it, reaches further and further into earthly consciousness.

You are all lifting each other day by day now, and the result is becoming unmistakable. Continue. Continue. Continue. We shall also continue our loving support in all ways possible.

* * * * * * * * * *

We would begin this message by returning to a topic that we mentioned a few days ago. The topic of flow has been given to you, our channel, both in session and in your own life, repeatedly over the last week and more. It is time now for you to expand upon the topic further than you have done in these messages. We know that we began once before and allowed the message to end before this picture was completed, but as you must realize by now, we try to keep these to short and easily digested portions.

You have been given the vision of a meeting, in council, of your self in dream state, others of your soul family, your Higher Self, guides, teachers, and divine beings. You have been led to understand that this is a planning committee that has been, is, and will continue to be in session throughout all time. This is where you participate, even initiate, the decisions which guide your lives. And this, dear friend, is where what you call flow originates.

Please understand that what we are describing to you is not, as you say, cast in stone. It is made with your input, and it can be changed the same way. However, in this game or play you have designed, maximum benefit is derived if you play your part without full recall of the process. Therefore, it seems to you, in your waking state, as if things happen **to you** when they do, in fact, happen **for you**. And, as you have so recently experienced, a seemingly miraculous thing occurs when you place your foot upon the path which most closely aligns with your chosen life contract. You move into the flow.

Understand that, from the moment you sign on to accomplish certain things for yourself and others, every available resource begins to create the conditions for your success. The skids, as you call them, have been greased. "How do I know what I need to do?" is the question we hear constantly. And the answer is, "Make a move, even if it is just mental." Examine all of the options you can think of, even the ones which seem impossible. Often enough, what seems impossible is only what you have not examined closely enough or that which, for some reason, you fear. Find out which seems to you to most feel right. What fills your heart with joy?

What makes you eager to start? Do not assign it to the impossible pile just yet.

Remember, the skids of the path you designed are greased. Now! Take a step, any step. The flow we are speaking about is the flow of life. You are in it with your canoe and paddle. When you take that first step, you will notice your canoe's reaction to the flow. If you are moving with your flow, your canoe will shoot forward and the apparent obstacles will fly past. If, however, you move in less than the optimal direction, it will seem as if you are trying to paddle upstream and your paddle has become a teaspoon. If you choose to sit in the stream and not do something... well, we think the picture is now clear enough, is it not?

The energy field in which you now sit, strengthening every moment now, will make it possible for you to accomplish far more, in far less time, than has been the case on your planet for many, many lifetimes, and is reaching a level never seen before. As more dear souls begin to awaken, these words and the truth in them will become more apparent. We recommend that you not wait for that. There is nothing holding you back but yourselves.

Look at the bright and divine soul that you are and step forth. Allow the past to be past and set your face to the future. Build that for yourselves. We will walk with you each step of the way.

Acknowledgments

I would like to thank the following people, all of whom I consider good friends, without whom this book would never have been written. First came April Colon who taught me ThetaHealing® and began my journey into the world of expanded consciousness. Suzanne Spooner taught me her TAUK method and thus started my opening to becoming a channel. Dolores Cannon, now in spirit, whose teachings of Quantum Healing Hypnosis Therapy have led me into further explorations of reality. Paul Selig and his guides have put me on a journey which I trust will never come to an end. Annette Despain has put much effort into the compilation of these messages, as has Alexis Winsor. Rick and Alexis Winsor have opened their home and hearts to me, giving the peace and space to do this. Thank you each for all you have contributed.

The Wisdom of Michael

About the Author

Ron spent 12 years in the U.S. Air Force, returning to civilian life in 1970. He entered a career in business after leaving the military which eventually found him managing the purchasing operations for several retail and wholesale companies. He was instrumental in revising the computer use of those companies to include their purchasing functions. After retiring in 2006 he is at last able to devote much more time to inner work, studying energy healing and opening up to the greater possibilities that have resulted in the channeling of this material. He now lives in Central Oregon. You will find his continuing work on http://www.oraclesandhealers.wordpress.com or on Facebook's Oracles and Healers page.

Made in the USA
San Bernardino, CA
20 February 2018